T0001662

MAL TA& GOZO

Travel with Marco Polo
Insider Tips

INSIDER TIP
Your shortcut
to a great
experience

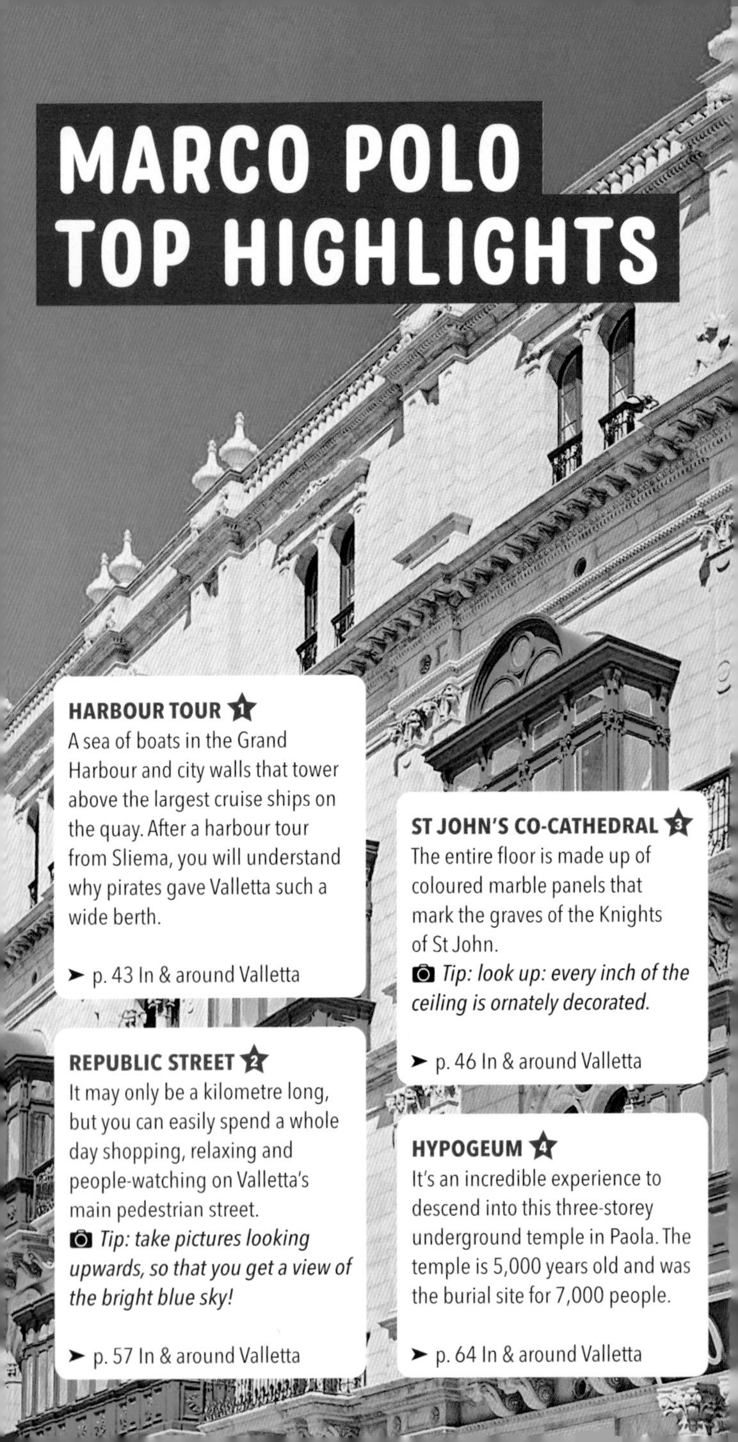

MARCO POLO TOP HIGHLIGHTS

HARBOUR TOUR ⭐

A sea of boats in the Grand Harbour and city walls that tower above the largest cruise ships on the quay. After a harbour tour from Sliema, you will understand why pirates gave Valletta such a wide berth.

➤ p. 43 In & around Valletta

REPUBLIC STREET ⭐2

It may only be a kilometre long, but you can easily spend a whole day shopping, relaxing and people-watching on Valletta's main pedestrian street.

📷 *Tip: take pictures looking upwards, so that you get a view of the bright blue sky!*

➤ p. 57 In & around Valletta

ST JOHN'S CO-CATHEDRAL ⭐3

The entire floor is made up of coloured marble panels that mark the graves of the Knights of St John.

📷 *Tip: look up: every inch of the ceiling is ornately decorated.*

➤ p. 46 In & around Valletta

HYPOGEUM ⭐

It's an incredible experience to descend into this three-storey underground temple in Paola. The temple is 5,000 years old and was the burial site for 7,000 people.

➤ p. 64 In & around Valletta

CATACOMBS ⭐7
Below modern-day Rabat lie great cities of the dead. It's a bit creepy to picture that, in ancient times, celebratory feasts were held in among the graves.

➤ p. 87 Central Malta

FONTANELLA TEA GARDEN ⭐8
Sit on Mdina's bastion with half the island at your feet and indulge in one of Fontanella's heavenly cakes.

➤ p. 89 Central Malta

MARSAXLOKK ⭐5
This is the only place on Malta where you'll find a romantic Mediterranean harbour, full of colourful fishing boats, which means it's the perfect place to eat fresh fish.

📷 *Tip: zoom in on the village church to create the perfect background for the brightly coloured boats.*

➤ p. 74 Southeast Malta

GHAJN TUFFIEHA BAY ⭐9
Paradise found! No beachfront road, no hotel, no sports – just a beach bar, fine sand, clear sea and, usually, very few people.

➤ p. 103 Northwest Malta

HAGAR QIM/MNAJDRA ⭐6
A Stone Age temple is enough of an attraction, but this one stands in splendid isolation surrounded by fields, with a long-range view over the Mediterranean.

📷 *Tip: the roof canopy prevents you getting a full shot of the temple; place someone in the entrance to get a sense of the immense scale of the structure.*

➤ p. 76 Southeast Malta

CITTADELLA ⭐10
An authentic ancient settlement with narrow alleyways, plenty of nature and only two restaurants. There are absolutely no cars here and no tourist souvenirs.

📷 *Tip: wait at the city gate until a monk or a priest makes an appearance.*

➤ p. 111 Gozo

CONTENTS

GOZO

NORTHWEST MALTA

IN & AROUND VALLETTA

CENTRAL MALTA

SOUTHEAST MALTA

CONTENTS

🕐   Plan your visit

€–€€€ Price categories

(*) Premium-rate
     phone number

🍴   Eating/drinking

🛍   Shopping

🍸   Going out

🏖   Top beaches

☂   Rainy day activities

🐝   Budget activities

👪   Family activities

🚩   Classic experiences

(*A2*) Refers to the removable pull-out map
(*a2*) Refers to the inset street map on the pull-out map
(0) Located off the map

BEST OF MALTA & GOZO

St Peter's Pool

BEST

WHEN IT RAINS

ACTIVITIES TO BRIGHTEN YOUR DAY

JOURNEY BACK IN TIME

There are countless audiovisual shows vying for your custom, but the best by far is *Malta Experience*. Great music, impressive visuals and good commentaries bring Malta's history entertainingly to life.

➤ p. 50, In & around Valletta

ART IN THE FORTRESS

The elegant stairway of *St James Cavalier* is a sight to behold. Upstairs you'll find modern art, an arthouse cinema and a small, intimate theatre that stages thought-provoking performances.

➤ p. 53, In & around Valletta

CITY SHOPPING

You won't find a host of exciting shopping malls on little Malta. Only *The Point* comes close to an international standard, with 50 shops and numerous designer brands (photo).

➤ p. 58, In & around Valletta

FISH-SPOTTING

You may recognise some of the fish that swim around the *National Aquarium* in St Paul's Bay from your dinner plate, but many others, including sharks and giant rays, are normally only seen by deep-sea divers. As an added bonus, there are exotic snakes on display.

➤ p. 102, Northwest Malta

GOING UNDERGROUND

The *Ghar Dalam cave* offers shelter when it rains. At a depth of 200m / 656ft you'll encounter the bones of prehistoric wolves, foxes and even dwarf elephants that once lived here.

➤ p. 76, Southeast Malta

HOLLYWOOD ON MALTA

Prefer the bright lights of Hollywood to the dark clouds of a rainy day? Then you'll enjoy the widest choice of films at the *Eden Century Cinema Complex*.

➤ p. 62, In & around Valletta

BEST 🐷
ON A BUDGET

FOR SMALLER WALLETS

THE KIOSKS OF ST PAUL'S BAY
You'll find them all over Malta, but the best ones are at St Paul's Bay: large kiosks with simple tables and stools on the beachfront promenade, where you can eat and drink in a laidback setting at an affordable price. The name of the *Harmony Kiosk* says it all. Sit among the greenery with a view of the sea and forget about the rest of the world – just like the locals do. *Triq it-Trunciera*
➤ p. 102, Northwest Malta

CHECK OUT THE BAKERY
The Maltese get themselves little delicacies from the bakery and then find a park bench or low-lying wall on which to enjoy them. Bakeries don't just sell sweet treats; you'll also find *pastizzi* – traditional, local pastries filled with meat, cheese or vegetables (photo) – and (less authentic) pizza slices.
➤ p. 27

DREAM TICKET
Do you like exploring? If you want to travel around the island without a hire car, then buy a *Tallinja Card Explore*. For just 21 euros (15 euros for children) you can use all the buses on Malta and Gozo as often as you like.
➤ p. 137

TWO-FOR-ONE OFFERS
The *Malta Discount Card* entitles you to heaps of two-for-one offers. It costs just 20 euros and is valid for ten days.
➤ p. 140

PARTY FOR FREE
Among partygoers, Paceville has a reputation as one of the nightlife hotspots of the central Mediterranean – and yet you don't have to pay a cover charge, even at the big night clubs, such as *Havana*.
➤ p. 63, In & around Valletta

BEST WITH CHILDREN

FUN FOR YOUNG AND OLD

PLAYMOBIL WORLD

Where do Playmobil figures come from? To find out, go direct to the production site. If you book in advance, you can tour the factory. And, if you don't book, you can still play with the figures for hours in the *Playmobil Fun Park* (photo). *Sun–Thu 10am–6pm, Fri/ Sat 10am–10pm | Admission 1.20 euros, children 2.40 euros, tours 8.50 euros per person | Hal Far | playmobilmalta.com | ⮽ M11*

SPLASH AND SLIDE

When splashing in the sea gets boring, families head for the *Splash & Fun* waterpark. The four giant slides are a big hit, and the pool's wave machine ensures that you can bathe safely in a swell, unlike in the sea. *Mid-May–mid-Sept (depending on the weather) daily 9am–8pm | admission 22 euros, children 15 euros | White Rocks | Bahar Ic-Caghaq | tel. 21 37 42 83 | splashandfunmalta.com | ⮽ K6*

FOR YOUNG SCIENTISTS

Are you ready to take a journey through the human intestine? Have you ever dreamt of firing up a hot air balloon, making your own firework or playing a harp without strings? It's all possible at Malta's new Science Centre; kids love it – and the grown-ups will have fun too. *Tue–Thu 9.30am–4pm, Fri 10.30am–5pm, Sat 10.30am–5pm, Sun 11.30am–6pm | admission depending on the extent of the visit 6–15 euros, children (4–11 years) 3–10 euros | Villa Bighi | Kalkara | es-plora.org.mt | ⮽ N8*

SHOCK HORROR

Malta's horror stories are true and, therefore, only suitable for older children: in the courtroom and in the old dungeons of the *Inquisitor's Palace* in Vittoriosa the darkest chapters of Malta's history are laid bare: torture and executions, war and the Inquisition. ➤ p. 67, In & around Valletta

BEST

CLASSIC EXPERIENCES

ONLY ON MALTA

OH, HOW LOVELY!

The only place to find a properly staged, photogenic folklore show in modern Malta is at *Ta' Marija* in Mosta, where the entertainment is accompanied by a good Maltese meal. Sometimes, there's dancing too.

➤ p. 94, Central Malta

DELICATE SILVER JEWELLERY

The Maltese are true masters of delicate silverwork, which makes a lovely souvenir. A good place to buy it is the *Silversmith's Shop* in Valletta.

➤ p. 58, In & around Valletta

MIDDAY GUN SALUTE

The Maltese make a great deal of their military history, so don't be alarmed when you hear the historic cannons of the *Saluting Battery* boom their midday salute right underneath the *Upper Barracca Gardens*. Be punctual or you'll miss it.

➤ p. 51, In & around Valletta

FIREWORKS EVERY WEEKEND

The Maltese love fireworks of all kinds, and there are 25 factories on the island catering for this craze. Nearly every weekend there's a firework display in one of the villages as part of a local festival (photo). Don't miss the chance to soak up the atmosphere.

➤ p. 141

POLITICAL ASSOCIATION OR BAND CLUB

Nearly every town and village has four special bars: two that are aligned to the island's two political parties and two that are typical Maltese *band clubs*. Newcomers are welcome, and the prices are accessible to all. If you enter one of the political bars, just make sure you know whether it's red or blue, to avoid any awkwardness.

➤ p. 111, Gozo

GET TO KNOW MALTA & GOZO

Carnival on Gozo

DISCOVER MALTA & GOZO

At Xwejni Bay on Gozo, the coastal limestone has weathered into wild rock formations

Malta is tiny but has a little bit of everything: cliffs and beaches, lively towns and quiet villages, plenty of art and 5,000 years of history. The calendar is full of events, and you can get around easily and cheaply on the comprehensive bus service. A holiday here is a city, beach and activity break rolled into one – and it's available all year round.

FASTEN YOUR SEAT BELTS, PLEASE!

Your plane starts its descent just off the south coast of Sicily. Ships ply the waters below as you pass Gozo, Malta's little sister island, and then, just like that, you're flying over Malta. If southerly winds prevail, your plane will touch down immediately. If the wind is blowing from the north, your pilot will circle over the sea

5200–2500 BCE
Stone Age settlers construct temples around 4000 BCE

2000–1000 BCE
Bronze Age residents cut mysterious tracks in stone

1000 BCE
Phoenician rule on Malta

218 BCE–CE 397
Roman rule on Malta

397–1070
Byzantine rule on Malta
Arab rule from 870

1070–1530
Conquered by the Normans from Sicily, then by the Hohenstaufen dynasty, and then by the Spanish kingdom of Aragón

between Malta and Africa before landing.

MUCH MORE THAN SEA

The journey to your hotel will take you around one roundabout after another. To discover Malta's greener side, you'll have to tour the island's far north and west – or take a trip to Gozo. First, check in to your hotel, and then set about exploring the island. It's easy to orientate yourself – just follow the water's edge. Joggers run laps along the wide promenades, pensioners sit on the many benches, posh Maltese take their ornamental, over-bred dogs for walkies and children enjoy the seafront play parks and swing themselves up into the blue skies above. English-language students of all nationalities populate the street-side cafés, and small groups of Maltese teenagers flock to the nearest McDonald's. Buses drive past virtually every minute; almost all of them heading to or from the fortified capital, Valletta. From there, they shuttle passengers to all the main historical and cultural sights around the island: 5,000-year-old Neolithic temples, the enormous catacombs at Rabat, the tranquil city of Mdina and the stunning natural beauty of the Dingli Cliffs. There are enough attractions on the island to fill a full week's holiday.

HEAVENLY SPLENDOUR

Top of many must-see lists are the magnificent churches that dot both islands. Every village has been striving for centuries to build a bigger and better church than their neighbouring community, with the result that the small town of Mosta has the fourth

1530–1798
The Knights of St John are awarded the islands

1565
Turkish siege of Malta

1800–1964
British rule

1940–42
German and Italian planes bombard the island

1964
Malta gains independence; a republic is declared in 1974

2004
Malta joins the EU; euro currency introduced in 2008

2018
Valletta named European Capital of Culture

largest church dome in the world, and Xewkija on Gozo has the third highest in Europe. Malta is also home to some of the world's most colourful church floors: knights and local nobility are buried under brightly coloured marble slabs in the cathedrals of Valletta and Mdina. This staunchly Roman Catholic island republic also has a record number of statues of popes. The Maltese are passionate about statues in all shapes and forms, even though most are made from papier-mâché and are only brought out for village festivals, or *festas*, when they are paraded on floats or carried by members of the congregation through streets lined with flags. The island's 25 firework factories ensure that these religious celebrations go off with a bang.

MONEY TALKS

The influence of the Catholic Church has waned since Malta became a member of the European Union in 2004. Since then, the country has learnt to profit from the advantages of membership. International wealth management and online gambling are booming sectors of the island's economy, and have attracted more than 10,000 international workers to Malta to manage vast amounts of money and to earn very high salaries for themselves. The lucrative effects of globalisation are clearly visible on Malta. An increasing number of cafés, bars and first-class restaurants now animate the social scene. The development of this small country took another leap forward in 2018 when Valletta was named European Capital of Culture.

TAKE IT EASY

The Maltese are avid fans of classic cars and 'sulkies' (lightweight, horse-drawn carriages). Joe from Gzira has his own yacht repair yard but is also the proud owner of 40 classic convertibles in a variety of models, all in mint condition. Every day after work, he spends two to three hours cruising across the island; virtually nobody overtakes him since 80kmph / 50mph is the speed limit, even on the island's four-lane motorways. In contrast, Bill from Kercem loves horses. He spends a few hours every day out on Malta's country roads in his sulky. For him, this is like taking a holiday. The Maltese rarely spend their holidays abroad anyway; they prefer buying a second home on their own island, right by the sea.

PARTY AROUND THE CAMPFIRE

Although sandy beaches can only be found in the north of Malta and Gozo, the Maltese don't need sand to enjoy the sea. They flock to the flat, rocky shores on summer weekends for picnics. Weighed down with barbecues, crates of drinks and camping chairs, large groups of families and friends head to the seaside to enjoy spending the day together. Some stay until the evening, listening to music around the campfire, but by midnight all is quiet. Those looking to party until the early hours go to Paceville and the nightclubs near Mdina. People on Malta are simply very considerate and respectful of others, and that's what makes a holiday on Malta and Gozo so relaxing.

AT A GLANCE

431,000
Population

Bristol: 466,000

**33km /
20.5 miles**
Greatest distance
between two towns on Malta

**25km /
15.5 miles**
Coastline (Malta and Gozo)
Coastline of mainland Great Britain:
17,819 km / 11,072 miles

**316km² /
122 sq miles**
Area
Isle of Wight: 380 km² /
147 sq miles

HIGHEST POINT

Ta' Dmejrek

**253m /
830ft**

WARMEST MONTH

AUGUST

31°C / 88°F

**MOST POPULAR
MONTH FOR TOURISTS**

JULY

9 UNESCO WORLD HERITAGE SITES

The seven temples — older than the Egyptian pyramids;
the subterranean Hypogeum; and the capital city of
Valletta in its entirety.

VALLETTA

With a population of just 5,680, this is
the smallest capital city in the EU.

ALLAH
is used to refer to the
Christian God in the Maltese
language.

TRADITIONAL FISHING BOATS
known as *luzzi* are only
allowed in the water if they
have eyes painted on their
bows.

UNDERSTAND MALTA & GOZO

character, as they are built with the local coral limestone that is surface-mined on Malta and Gozo, then cut and transported to the construction sites by truck. Closed-down quarries, meanwhile, are being used to store the rubble from demolished old buildings.

BINGO!

Maltese housewives and pensioners have always enjoyed their bingo nights held at *band clubs* and community halls. Betting on the horses at the race course in Marsa is also a popular pastime. Serious money can be won and lost playing roulette and blackjack in Malta's casinos. The big winner on Malta, however, is the online gambling (or iGaming) industry, which now employs more than 9,000 people on the island; what's more, over 1,000 students have signed up for courses at the iGaming Academy since 2017. Along with Gibraltar, Malta is Europe's centre for global online gambling.

BUILDING BOOM

Strolling through the streets in the evening, you will notice a large number of empty flats in many of the old buildings. The idea of living in these ancient, crumbling houses has lost its appeal. A newly built house outside the centre is usually cheaper than a complete renovation, which is why many locals are relocating. Most of the old buildings now only house a ground-floor shop at most. This is why Malta's towns are spreading across the island, and its villages are merging into one another. Yet the new houses still retain some of the traditional

LESSONS IN THE SUN

Who likes learning under perpetual grey skies and heavy rain? Language holidays in the Mediterranean are far more appealing. Malta has become

the perfect destination for students of English. More than 80,000 students a year come to Malta from all over the world to be taught the Queen's English by local language teachers. There are more than 40 accredited language schools to choose from, and they are responsible for creating well-paid jobs on the island. Most of the schools are situated between Sliema and St Julian's, but Gozo also offers courses.

MALTESE KNIGHTS

Just who were the knights who left their fortifications all over Malta? They were drawn from all over Europe and were often the second or third sons of noble families, who had little to inherit and so looked to make their fortune abroad.

become knights, but first they had to complete a two-year probationary period as novices: one year caring for the sick, another fighting on a galley.

The order was subdivided into a number of national groupings known as *langues* (tongues). The Grand Master of the Order was chosen for life by a committee of electors, and all knights owed absolute obedience to him. He also represented the Order in external affairs, just like the ruler of a nation state.

History everywhere: a relic from recent British rule meets a Maltese cross

The Military Hospitaller Order of Saint John of Jerusalem, known for short as the Knights of St John or the Knights Hospitaller, was founded in 1099, following the conquest of Jerusalem, by participants in the First Crusade. Only noblemen could

In order to finance an organisation like this, the Knights Hospitaller received donations from European rulers and revenue from their possessions all over the continent; if this was insufficient, they did not shrink from piracy to supplement their income.

TRUE OR FALSE?

MALTA IS STRICTLY CATHOLIC

That's true. Ninety per cent of Maltese are Roman Catholic, and the number of priests per head of population is only exceeded by the Vatican: out of every 614 baptised children, one will go on to become a priest. Young boy scouts still roam the beaches and hotel pools asking topless female sunbathers to cover up, so that they don't corrupt the Maltese youth. That said, the influence of the church has waned since Malta joined the EU in 2004. In 2011, over half the population voted to allow divorce, and in 2017 the Maltese parliament passed a law to legalise same-sex marriage.

EVERYONE SPEAKS ENGLISH

Not far off. Certainly, English is the language of tourism, but you'll find that most locals prefer to speak Maltese *(Malti)* between themselves. Maltese can be hard for English-speakers to understand as it is more closely related to Arabic than to other European languages. Street names can be particularly confusing: some use the English version; others, the Maltese. Some places even have two names: Senglea, for example, is now officially known as L-Isla, while Vittoriosa is also called Birgu. In such cases, guesswork and intuition may help you out.

DRINKING SEAWATER

You can go thirsty, even on an island. Malta is one of the ten countries worldwide with the lowest supply of drinking water, almost on a par with the states on the Arabian peninsula. Aside from the island's breweries and wineries, help is also on hand from the island's seawater desalination plants, which produce more than half of the 30 million m^3 of drinking water that flows from taps and showers. Seawater desalination accounts for almost four per cent of the country's electricity consumption. Despite this outlay, the island's tap water still tastes disgusting, so the Maltese continue to import bottled water from Italy, Wales and Scotland.

SET IN STONE

If you're ever asked to define the words megalith (literally, large stone) and neolith (new stone), picture in your mind's eye the ancient temples on Malta and Gozo. They were built in the Neolithic Period (the New Stone Age), five to six thousand years ago, and their construction was an amazing feat of engineering. Gigantic slabs of stone, known as megaliths, were moved on stone rollers from the quarries to the construction sites, where earthworks were used to raise them up into a vertical position.

The largest megalith was 4m / 13ft high, 7m / 20ft long, 60cm / 24 in thick and weighed more than 20 tons. There are two other words that may help you understand the information provided at the temple sites: an orthostat is a slab-like stone set in a vertical

Stone on stone: immense megaliths were used in the construction of Hagar Qim

or upright position; when a third horizontal stone is laid across two supporting orthostats, the resulting structure is known as a trilithon.

ON TRACK

You could be forgiven for thinking that the earliest inhabitants of Malta were slightly crazy. First, they carried gigantic slabs of stones around the island. Then they gouged hundreds, if not thousands, of parallel lines into the rock to resemble railway tracks, even though the wheel hadn't been invented yet. They dug out numerous crossings and junctions, and even a kind of railway interchange, now aptly known as *Clapham Junction*. Remains of these tracks, some up to 40 cm / 15 in deep, can be found at 150 sites on Malta and Gozo. The most popular theory is that, 3,500 years ago, humans and animals pulled heavy carts along these ancient grooves. But no one knows for certain where they were going, or why.

NEW LABOUR

The face of Malta is changing as a result of poverty and war around the world. Since 2002, 19,000 refugees have arrived on the island by boat, mainly from Libya, Syria, Eritrea and Somalia. Six thousand of them now have legal resident status on the island, though they're still outnumbered by British ex-pats. Life can be hard for these new arrivals; many work in low-paid manual jobs as refuse collectors, road cleaners, construction workers or labourers transporting heavy gas bottles.

SPONSOR A TREE

If trees could speak, they would be crying out for help on Malta. The island has a drastic shortage of trees, with very few growing outside the main towns. The landscape is dominated by dry scrubland, where only thyme, rosemary, heather, spurge and alliums grow.

The *Gaia Foundation (www.projectgaia.org)* is committed to re-forestation, and you can help them by sponsoring a tree. If trees are too quiet for you, why not sponsor a kitten instead *(www.animalcaremalta.com)*?

DEVIL'S TIME

A word of caution before checking the time on a church tower clock in Malta: almost every second clock stands still or shows the wrong time. This is no coincidence. It is done to confuse Satan so that he doesn't turn up and disturb the mass. Sometimes the clock faces are not even real but are merely painted on for decoration. If a church has two towers and therefore two clocks, only one will show the correct time.

HUNTING BIRDS

There are around 16,000 hunters on Malta, who kill migratory birds with nets and guns. Stone shelters for the hunters and piles of stones for the cages of decoy birds can be seen all over the countryside.

Malta's accession to the EU and the good work of *BirdLife Malta (birdlifemalta.org)* have brought about some important changes in recent years. Setting traps is now prohibited. The spring hunt has been banned, and the autumn hunt has been restricted to target only 32 out of the 384 species of migrating birds that visit Malta. Nevertheless, some Maltese continue to hunt illegally, shooting birds of prey and herons, in particular, as trophies to display in their taxidermy collections at home.

CRIMES & MISDEMEANOURS

In 2017, investigative journalist Daphne Caruana Galizia was killed by a car bomb close to her home on Malta. Her death made international headlines. In fact, since 2010 there have been 20 such attacks, resulting in a total of five deaths; however, most involved members of organised crime, and in no cases were holidaymakers affected. The annual murder rate remains in single digits – something an average Scandi thriller would achieve in 90 minutes. Other violent crimes are just as rare, and even the number of pickpocketing incidents is under a thousand. The bottom line is that, as a tourist, you can feel much safer in Malta and Gozo than in countless other countries.

SATISFIED WITH EUROPE

After World War II, the Maltese preferred to remain a colony of the United Kingdom rather than become an independent country. Today, they are among the happiest Europeans, along with the Lithuanians, Latvians and Irish: 84 per cent think that the EU is a good idea and are glad to be part of it.

A shrine to murdered journalist Daphne Caruana Galizia

This is in stark contrast to the UK, which voted to leave the EU in 2016. Malta's enthusiasm for the EU is reflected in the polls: three-quarters of all Maltese citizens voted in the last European elections – only Belgium and Luxembourg recorded a higher turnout.

EARNING ENOUGH?

The minimum adult wage on Malta is 169.76 euros a week. The Prime Minister earns 980 euros a week, while the State President takes home 1,076 euros. As a comparison, consider that Bill Gates could easily spend 442 million euros a week. Yet you do not hear the Maltese complaining about their incomes, because the country's unemployment rate is low and the economy is stable.

TAX HAVEN

Legal, but not entirely ethical: Malta's tax system operates within EU legislation as a paradise for multinationals and rich individuals. Hundreds of Maltese tax lawyers work almost exclusively for wealthy European clients who purchase their yachts here to save heavily on sales tax. Offshore jurisdictions are used by many large UK companies, which register on Malta to pay as little as five per cent tax on their profits.

EATING
SHOPPING
SPORT

Souvenir magnets

EATING & DRINKING

Top chef Jamie Oliver raved about the portion sizes served in Maltese restaurants. The range of cuisine on offer doesn't disappoint either.

A CULINARY WORLD TOUR

Despite ruling the island for almost 150 years, the British left very few traces of their influence on the island's cuisine – apart from the full English breakfast, that is, which is served everywhere on Malta until well after noon. Otherwise, the restaurant scene is dominated by Italian and, especially, Sicilian cuisine. Many of the chefs working on Malta come from Italy, so authenticity is guaranteed. Pizza and homemade pasta are served everywhere, alongside regional specialities from all parts of Italy. In general, there has been a noticeable trend in recent years towards more gourmet establishments with prices to match. Non-European restaurants and atmospheric wine bars are also growing in popularity.

If you are so inclined, you can take a culinary trip around the world on Malta, with destinations ranging from Greece and the Middle East to Malaysia, Indonesia, India, China, Mongolia and Japan.

MALTESE FLAVOURS

After long years of neglect, the availability of Maltese specialities has greatly improved. These include a great variety of soups and casseroles, rabbit recipes and vegetable dishes. The national dish on Malta is *fenek*, which consists of rabbit, usually served in a garlic and red wine sauce. Malta was long dependent on cheap imported olive oil from Italy, but good restaurants are now cooking with genuine Maltese olive oil once again, as the cultivation of olives on the island has taken an upward turn.

Bruschetta

The Maltese are also keen on cakes, tarts and pastries, which are sold in any number of *confectionery shops*. Look out too for typical Maltese *pastizzi*, rolls or pockets of pastry stuffed with a variety of fillings, from pureed peas to cream cheese. A *pastizzerija* will have a particularly good selection and will usually also sell small portions of *timpana*, baked pasta in a pastry case.

> **INSIDER TIP**
> **Hide and seek in pastry**

Another very popular sweet speciality, sold mostly at church festivals and markets, is *helwa tat-tork;* this is a nougat made of sugar and almonds, similar to Turkish halva.

GONE FISHING

Fish is an ever-present staple on Maltese menus. However, half the fish sold on the islands is imported deep-frozen. If you want to eat some really fresh fish, it's best to go to a good restaurant where the whole fish is on display. The price will then depend on the weight. Octopus stew, cooked in red wine, is a popular, low-cost seafood dish. From August to November, the most popular fresh fish is *lampuki*, which is similar to mackerel and has firm white flesh. It is steamed, grilled, baked, fried or served as a casserole, *torta tal lampuki*, with pureed cauliflower, onions and tomatoes. Swordfish is always a tasty option and, what's more, it's free of little bones. Steer clear of calamari and shrimps, as they are almost always imported frozen from halfway across the world .

QUENCH YOUR THIRST

Malta has no recognised national drink, although milk, fruit juice, wine, beer, several kinds of liqueur and three types of *kinnie* – a bitter fizzy

Delicious! Almond and carob liqueurs

GOOD TO KNOW

Restaurant menus are always available in English. Most restaurants also put their food and drink menus, including the prices, on their websites, so you can whet your appetite before you arrive. In high-end restaurants the waiter will show you to your table. In some establishments, it is customary to sip an aperitif at the bar or in the lounge while you peruse the menu. The waiter will lead you to your table as soon as your starter is ready.

Meal times on Malta are similar to the UK. Lunch is usually served from noon until 2pm, dinner from 7pm to 10pm. Anyone who wants to make a more thorough study of the gastronomic scene on Malta should look out for *The Definitive(ly) Good Guide to Restaurants in Malta and Gozo*, which is updated annually and available from the island's bookshops. For the latest information, see also *restaurantsmalta.com*.

drink made from unpeeled oranges, water and vermouth – are all produced on the island. Beer comes largely from two breweries, Carlsberg and Farsons, although a number of craft breweries have also emerged in recent years. Wine from the barrel can only be found in simple village taverns nowadays. Restaurants usually stock international bottled wines, as the island's grape production comes nowhere near to meeting demand. Although Maltese winemakers have begun to import young vines of various types from France and Italy to plant on the island, it is still necessary for them to buy grapes, usually from Italy, in order to make enough "Maltese" wine to stock the island's cellars.

Fenek

Today's Recommendations

Starters

ALJOTTA
Fish soup with lots of garlic, herbs and rice

MINESTRA
Maltese version of the Italian mixed vegetable soup, served with fresh sheep's or goat's cheese

RAVJUL
Ravioli filled with Gozitan ricotta cheese

Main courses

BRAGIOLI
Roulade of beef, stuffed with egg, minced veal and peas

BRUGIEL MIMLI
Aubergines filled with rice, minced beef and herbs

ROSS FIL-FORN
Cheese-topped baked rice with minced beef, eggs and tomatoes

TIMPANA
Baked pasta – usually macaroni – with béchamel sauce and minced beef

Desserts

IMQARETS
Pastry rolls filled with chopped dates

BISKUTTINI TAL-LEWZ
Almond biscuits, usually baked on rice paper – perfect with coffee

KANNOLI
Crispy pastry rolls filled with cream cheese and candied fruits

Drinks

BAJTRA
Liqueur made from the fruit of the prickly pear cactus

GUZE PASSITO
A fine red dessert wine made from Shiraz grapes by the Marsovin winery

KINNIE
Bittersweet orange soda

SHOPPING

No one comes to Malta for the shopping. There are other destinations for that. Authentic Maltese souvenirs are in short supply, although you can find them if you know where to look. And an internet search may reveal good deals on international brands of trainers, clothing, jewellery and watches.

MULTI-COLOURED GLASS

The glass-blowers of Malta and Gozo have an international reputation for the high quality of their work. The vibrant colours of their creations are reminiscent of Venetian Murano glassware. A variety of colours and shapes are combined to create artistic and harmonious glasses, jugs, vases, candleholders and figures. Most of the glass-blowers can be found in *Ta' Qali* on Malta and in *San Lawrenz* on Gozo, where you can watch them at work on their beautiful creations.

TASTY DELICACIES

Maltese liqueurs bearing the name Zeppi's are colourful gifts to take home – and they taste good, too. They come in all sorts of exotic flavours, including prickly pear, almond, honey, pomegranate, fennel, carob and fig. Home cooks will want to buy supplies of Gozitan sea salt, pickled capers and sun-dried tomatoes, not to mention some highly prized Maltese olive oil. You'll find a good selection of culinary treats in the Departures area at the airport, including sweet stuff from *Café Cordina (244 Republic Street | Valletta)*.

MALTESE DESIGNERS

If you want to know what Malta's fashion designers are capable of, then visit

Maltese lace (left) and glassware (right)

during Fashion Week at the end of May/beginning of June. This is when they present their designs at individual catwalk shows in Fort St Elmo. At other times, you'll need to contact the designers directly through the website, *fashionweek.com.mt/*.

INSIDER TIP
Malta à la mode
Only one local label has so far dared to open a flagship store in Valletta: *Charles & Ron (58D Republic Street, underneath the Grand Master's Palace | charlesandron.com)*; it's worth window-shopping here at the very least.

FOR LITTLE KNIGHTS

There are some quirky Maltese souvenirs for children. Wooden swords for wannabe knights are, perhaps, to be expected, but in Ta' Qali you can buy an entire suit of armour made from tin plate. Easier to carry is the Playmobil

Grand Master of the Knights of St John – this figure is only available on Malta.

TRADITIONAL CRAFTS

For centuries, Maltese and, above all, Gozitan women have been making Maltese lace to adorn tablecloths, handkerchiefs, napkins, scarves and stoles. These industrious women also knit pullovers and caps. The best of their craftwork can be bought in Victoria and San Lawrenz on Gozo.

Maltese stone makes for a weightier, some might say cumbersome, souvenir. The local limestone is not only used to construct almost all the buildings on the island, but also to make items of everyday use such as ashtrays, and paperweights, as well as modern sculptures. If this is what you're looking for, go to Ta' Qali and *Limestone Heritage* in Siggiewi.

SPORT & ACTIVITIES

In all honesty, there are better destinations if you want a sporting holiday. Nevertheless, Malta has plenty of activities and facilities to keep you moving. The sea offers opportunities for a variety of watersports in the summer months, and diving is possible all year round, thanks to over 50 diving centres dotted around the islands. Hiking is another pleasurable pastime; Malta's modest size means that wherever you roam you are nearly always treated to views of the entire island

CLIMBING

Is it really possible to go climbing on Malta where the highest peak is just 253m / 830ft above sea level? You bet! There are over 1,500 routes to choose from, and most of them are along the coast, so you will have sea views while you climb. For a different perspective, try Sea Level Traversing (SLT). Traverse the rocky cliffs by clambering sideways, just above the waterline, and when you get tired, simply allow yourself to fall into the sea. One SLT specialist is *MC Adventure (½ day for 2 participants 130 euros, full day 190 euros | 150 Salvu Psaila Street | Birkirkara | tel. 99 47 03 77 | mcadventure.com.mt)*. For guided climbing on Gozo, try *Gozo Adventures (Tel. 99 99 45 92 | gozoadventures.com)*.

INSIDER TIP
Just let yourself fall

CYCLING

The streets between Valletta and St Julian's are hell for cyclists. This is why *EcoBikes Malta (8 Triq L-Imsell 8 | Bugibba | 2 mins from the main square | mountain bike from 15 euros/day, 90 euros/week; E-bikes 20 euros/day, 120 euros/week | tel. 27 50 00 22 | bikerentalmalta.com)*,

Climbing a rock face with waves crashing beneath you – the ultimate adrenalin kick

Malta's best bike rental agency, is located in Bugibba. From there, you'll be on smaller streets and within easy reach of more rural surroundings. For a fee, you can get your bike delivered to anywhere on the island; guided tours start from Bugibba. Gozo is a better destination for cyclists than Malta. Best bike rental on Gozo: *On Two Wheels (Triq ir-Rabat 36 | Marsalforn | tel. 21 56 15 03 | www.gozo.com/on2wheels).*

DIVING

With its clear water, wealth of marine life and interesting rock formations, Malta is a mecca for divers from all over Europe. There are tens of diving bases and schools offering their services to both beginners and advanced divers. The minimum age for diving lessons is 14; you'll need to bring a doctor's health certificate, either from home or from a doctor on Malta.

Here is a selection of diving schools on Malta:
Divemed (Zonqor Point | Marsaskala | tel. 21 63 99 81 | divemed.com); Madshark (at the Hotel Ambassador | St Paul's Bay | tel. 21 58 42 74 | madsharkmalta.com); Octopus Garden (at the Suncrest Hotel | Qawra | tel. 21 58 43 18 | and at the Gillieru Harbour Hotel | St Paul's Bay | tel. 21 57 87 25 | octopus-garden.com); Paradise Diving School (at the Paradise Bay Hotel | Cirkewwa | tel. 21 57 41 16 | paradisediving.com).

Here is a selection of diving schools on Gozo:
Calypso Diving Centre (Marsalforn | next to Hotel Calypso | tel. 21 56 17 57 | calypsodivers.com); Frankie's Gozo Diving Centre (Mgarr Road | Xewkija | tel. 21 55 13 15 | gozodiving.com); Nautic Team Gozo (Triq il Vulcan | Marsalforn | tel. 21 55 85 07 | nauticteam.com).

HIKING & RUNNING

There are several reasonably well-marked hiking trails on Malta and Gozo. The offices of the Malta Tourism Authority provide detailed descriptions of individual routes under the title *Country Walks* for approx. 2.50 euros per tour sheet.

The qualified and friendly guides at *Malta Nature Tours* will take you through the countryside of Malta and Gozo in small groups on a variety of full- and half-day adventures. Transport to the start of the walk is usually provided (*maltanaturetours.com*). Since 1986, an international marathon and a half marathon, open to all, have been held on Malta in mid to late February. The start is in Mdina, the finish in Sliema. Registration is through the Malta Tourism Authority, with information provided at *maltamarathon.com*.

HORSE RIDING

Golden Bay Horse Riding (Golden Bay | tel. 21 57 33 60 | goldenbayhorseriding.com) organises guided rides on the relatively secluded northwest coast. On Gozo, contact *Dreams of Horses Farm (Wied Ta L' Ghejun | Xaghra | tel. 2 15 59 22 29 | fb: @dreamsofhorsesfarm)*; you'll have to give two days' notice and provide the names of the riders in advance. They also rent out horse-drawn carriages and offer lessons in how to drive them.

KAYAKING

Gliding along the rocky coast of Malta and Gozo is a fantastic experience. A specialist for guided kayak tours, including transfers, is *Malta Rugged Coast Adventures (tours 65–75 euros incl. lunch; hire 10 euros/hr or 40 euros/day for a single kayak, 15 euros/hr, 50 euros/day for a double | in the Mellieha Bay Hotel | Ghadira | tel. 21 52 92 51 | www.seakayakmalta.com). Gozo Adventures (tel. 99 99 45 92 | gozoadventures.com)* offer tours around the coasts of Gozo and Comino. Experienced kayakers who want to go it alone can hire kayaks from *Xlendi Watersports (Xlendi | tel. 99 42 79 17 | gozoboathire.com)*.

SEGWAY

Can Segway riding really be classed as a sport? Try it for yourself and you will soon realise that you need a good sense of balance and body control. Guided tours on Segways are available through urban Valletta and along the Dingli Cliffs or on off-road trails along Golden Sands Beach with *Segway Malta (tel. 99 42 19 63 | segwaymalta.com)*.

On Gozo, you can join a five-hour cross-country tour of the island directly from the ferry port. Less strenuous and shorter tours can also be booked at *Gozo Segway Tours (tel. 99 42 19 63 | gozosegway.com)*. The prices on Gozo range from 15 to 90 euros, compared to between 45 and 60 euros on Malta.

WINDSURFING & OTHER WATERSPORTS

Mellieha Bay is by far the most popular location for all types and levels of windsurfing, and has two centres to cater for demand. If you bring your own equipment with you, you can windsurf off most of the island's coast. Experienced windsurfers book with the mobile surfing centre *Surfing Malta (Garaxx 4 | Carmela Dimech Street | Mosta | tel. 79 75 21 08 | surfingmalta.com)*, which changes its location every day to suit the wind conditions and also organises stand-up paddleboarding (SUP) and even yoga paddling. Kitesurfing can only be done if you have your own equipment.

There is a wide choice of motorised watersports available, ranging from jet-skiing to waterskiing; contact *Yellow Fun Water Sports (GT Court D Flat 18 | Jean de la Valette Street | St Paul's Bay | tel. 99 42 31 62 | fb: Yello Fun)* or *Sun 'n' Fun (Corinthia Marina Hotel | St George's Bay | tel. 21 37 38 22 | sunfunmalta.com)*.

You can get an adrenaline rush on Gozo by hiring a jet ski from *Xlendi Watersports (Tel. 99 42 79 17 | gozo-boathire.com)*. You can also hire motorboats without the need for a licence, as long as the sea is calm; you'll be given a short tutorial on navigating the island's steep coastline.

Explore reefs, wrecks and caves in the waters around Gozo and Comino

REGIONAL OVERVIEW

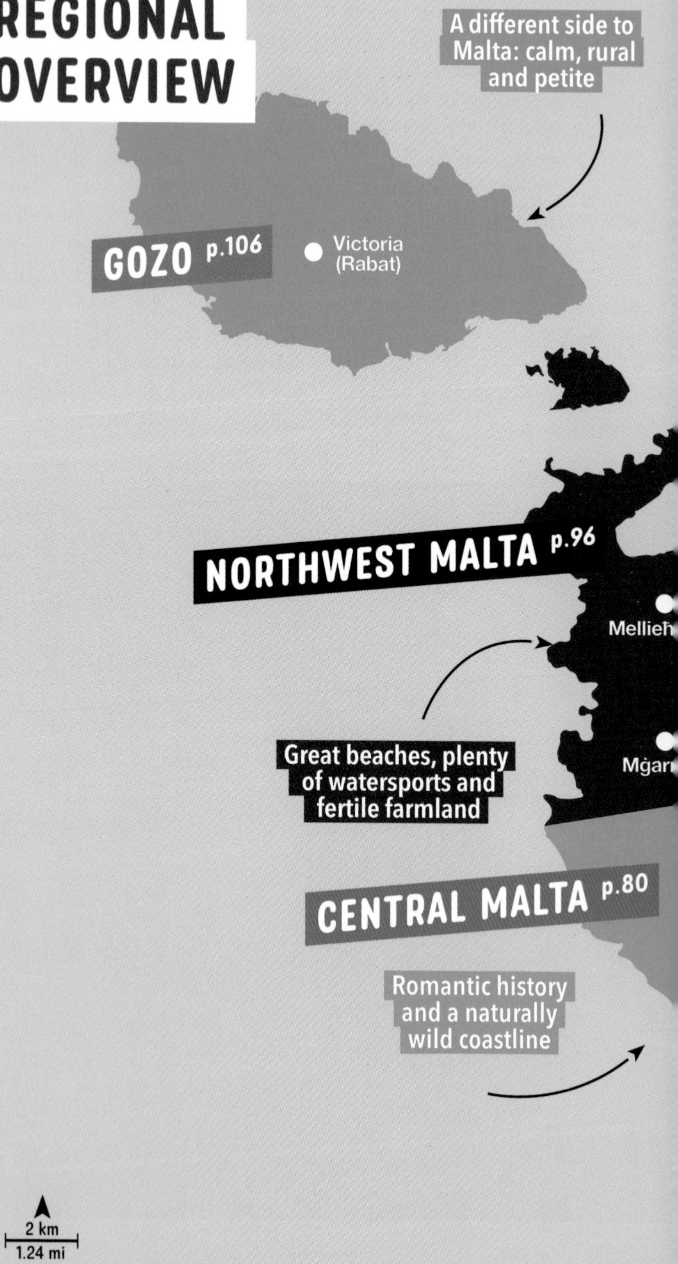

A different side to Malta: calm, rural and petite

GOZO p.106

● Victoria (Rabat)

NORTHWEST MALTA p.96

● Mellieħ

Great beaches, plenty of watersports and fertile farmland

CENTRAL MALTA p.80

● Mġarr

Romantic history and a naturally wild coastline

2 km
1.24 mi

MEDITERRANEAN SEA

Buġibba

IN & AROUND VALLETTA p.38

St. Julians

City break destination overlooking a huge harbour

Sliema

Valletta

Rabat

Hamrun

Vittoriosa

Luqa

Marsaxlokk

Żurrieq

SOUTHEAST MALTA p.70

Fishing boats, Stone Age temples and hardly a hotel to be seen

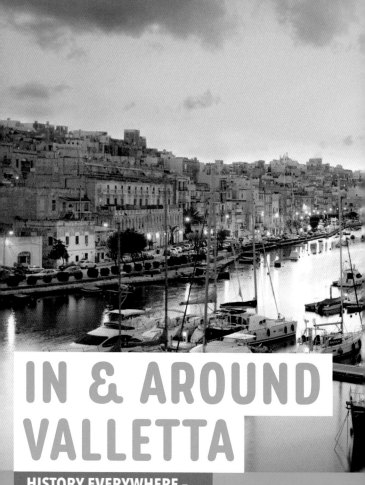

IN & AROUND VALLETTA

HISTORY EVERYWHERE – BUT PLENTY OF CAFÉS TOO

Half of Malta is a city. Or so it may appear to the majority of tourists and visitors to the island, who tend to stay in Valletta. This urban metropolis bursts with life, and its coastal location and seemingly endless number of bays make it an attractive destination. The city's pulse can be felt along the sweeping seafront promenades, which are dotted with cafés and bars, restaurants, marinas, hotels, pools and even a few bathing spots among the rocks.

Yachts fill Valletta's marina

To find your way around the city, start by studying the map inside the back cover. Although there seem to be numerous individual towns and suburbs on the edge of Valletta, the distinctions mean little to visitors. In reality, a single sea of houses stretches along the coast between Paceville, Floriana, the airport, Paola, Tarxien and Vittoriosa. The other dominant feature is water: the Grand Harbour, with its luxury yachts, rowing boats, cruise liners and container ships, lies right on the edge of the old town.

VALLETTA OLD TOWN

The Strand
Ix-Xatt ta' Tigné
The Point

17
Sliema Ferry

Habour tour ★

Marsamxett

Triq Marsamxett

Boat Street
S. Sebastian Street

Misrah Sant' Ierm

Triq Kristoforu
Triq l-Ifran
Triq ir-Repubblika

Strait Street 5
The Silversmith's Sh

Alchemy
Republic Street ★

Monaliza Valletta

Freedom Square 1
7 Casa Rocca Piccola

Manoel Theatre 6

Triq San Triq Zekka
Triq Santa Lucija
Strait – Street
Triq tat- Teatru l-Antik
Triq l-Arcisqof

Legligin
Blue Room

Triq Melita
Triq Nofs-in-Nhar
Triq l-Ifran

Anthony d'Amato
Angelica

4 Grand Master's Palace ★

St John's Co-Cathedral ★

National Museum of Archeology/
Auberge de Provence ★ 2

3
Agenda
Is Suq Tal-Belt

Triq il-Merkanti
Lower Barracca Gardens 1

Valletta Ditch

Wembley Store
City Gate
Charles Grech

14 MUZA

Triq San Pawl
Triq Sant'Orsola
Barriera Wharf

Café Society
Bridge Bar

St James Cavalier 16
15 Auberge de Castille, Léon e Portugal

Cassar

12 Upper Barracca Gardens/ Saluting Battery
13 Lascaris War Rooms

Triq Girolomu

Triq Sant'Anna

11 Cruise Terminal

Tarxien ★
Hypogeum ★

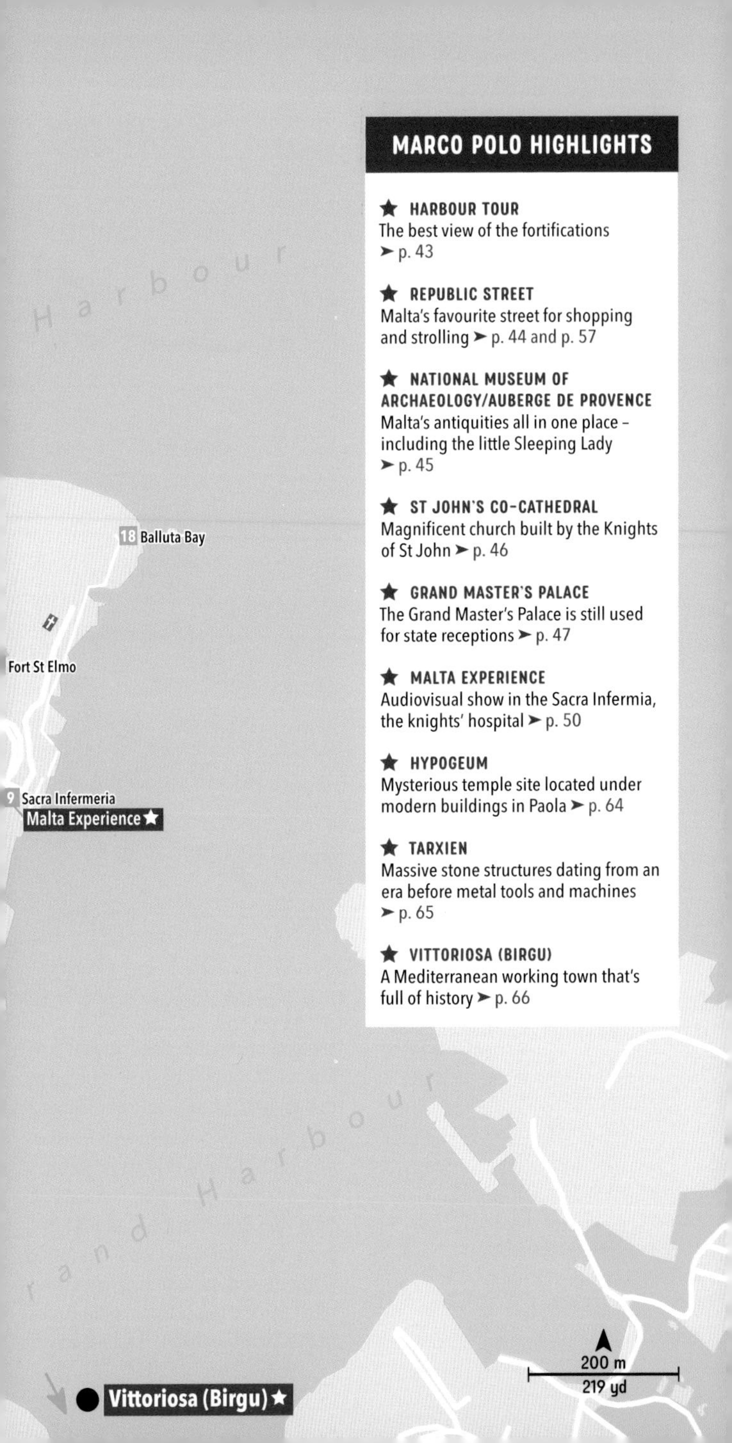

Balluta Bay 18

Fort St Elmo

Sacra Infermeria 9
Malta Experience ★

MARCO POLO HIGHLIGHTS

★ **HARBOUR TOUR**
The best view of the fortifications
➤ p. 43

★ **REPUBLIC STREET**
Malta's favourite street for shopping
and strolling ➤ p. 44 and p. 57

★ **NATIONAL MUSEUM OF
ARCHAEOLOGY/AUBERGE DE PROVENCE**
Malta's antiquities all in one place –
including the little Sleeping Lady
➤ p. 45

★ **ST JOHN'S CO-CATHEDRAL**
Magnificent church built by the Knights
of St John ➤ p. 46

★ **GRAND MASTER'S PALACE**
The Grand Master's Palace is still used
for state receptions ➤ p. 47

★ **MALTA EXPERIENCE**
Audiovisual show in the Sacra Infermia,
the knights' hospital ➤ p. 50

★ **HYPOGEUM**
Mysterious temple site located under
modern buildings in Paola ➤ p. 64

★ **TARXIEN**
Massive stone structures dating from an
era before metal tools and machines
➤ p. 65

★ **VITTORIOSA (BIRGU)**
A Mediterranean working town that's
full of history ➤ p. 66

Vittoriosa (Birgu) ★

200 m
219 yd

Only a few places are of interest to holidaymakers; between Valletta and Paceville to the north, the only real attraction is the coastline; the rest you can forget.

The area around the Grand Harbour gives a different picture altogether: the old cities of Valletta, Senglea and Vittoriosa each perch on their own rugged peninsula and offer their own romantic flair. You can spend a full holiday in Valletta and at least one afternoon and evening exploring Vittoriosa. Senglea is an excellent base for those who want to mix with the locals.

The inland towns of Paola and Tarxien attract culture enthusiasts with their Stone Age temples above and below ground. Buses shuttle passengers to the surrounding districts; passenger ferries also sail between the different harbours.

Five hundred years ago, when the Turks attempted to invade Malta, Vittoriosa and Senglea were the only

WHERE TO START?

Republic Street is the best place to start exploring Valletta. It begins at the new **Parliament Building** (*c4*) near the bus station, a five-minute walk from the ferry. It is not advisable to come into the city by car; instead take the ferry from Sliema or a bus from anywhere on the island. If you do drive, the best chance of a parking space is in the underground car park below the bus station.

settlements on the island. At that time, Malta had recently been conquered by the Knights of St John, who successfully fought back the Turkish invaders and built Valletta, the most fortified city in Europe, as a symbol of their victory. The British arrived around 200 years ago, and developed the Grand Harbour and surrounding coast area into the most important maritime base in the Mediterranean. The best way to

500 m
547 yd

Henry J. Beans

Casino Dragonara Palace

Lounge

Blackbull Pub

na

Avenue

La Maltija

no's

Gorg Borg Olivier

M e d i t e r r a n e a n

S e a

Triq it-Torri

Triq Sir Adrian Dingli

Neptune's Fresh Water Pool

Sliema Pitch

Guy's Bar Plough & Anchor Restaurant

Vecchia Napoli

Triq Sant'Elena

Triq il-Kbira

Mrabat

Le Malte

Triq Rodolfu

Triq Manwel Dimech

Harbour tour ★

17

Sliema Ferry

The Strand

The Strand

The Point

Triq San Albert

Triq D'Argens

Casey's Bar

get to know the harbour is to take a ★ *harbour tour* from Sliema – that's when you'll know you're on holiday in the Mediterranean and surrounded by history. The other districts around Valletta date from the post-war period.

During the day, the promenade at Sliema is in the liveliest area; in the evenings, crowds of partygoers flock to St Julian's and Paceville, especially on Fridays and Saturdays.

VALLETTA

(◻ M7) **What a transformation! A once lifeless administrative city full of churches and museums has been revitalised into a vibrant cultural capital with trendy bars, theatres and street cafés.**

Malta's capital (pop. 7,100) used to go to sleep at the close of business.

Nowadays, the city is still buzzing well after midnight. New people and businesses have breathed life into Valletta; a series of small boutique hotels has even opened in the city's old fortifications. The changes can be attributed

came from the Vatican and European ruling houses, so that , by the turn of the century, the fortified city of Valletta looked much as it does today. Within the mighty fortifications, the knights' palaces are still used today by the

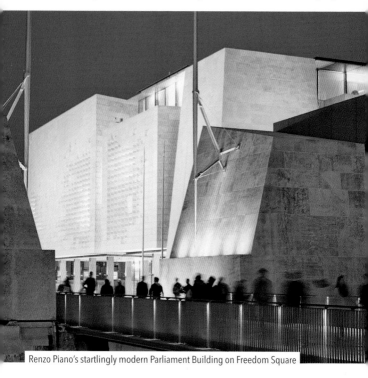

Renzo Piano's startlingly modern Parliament Building on Freedom Square

largely to the city's status as European Capital of Culture in 2018.

But culture is nothing new to this magnificent Baroque city. Before the Turkish siege of 1565, Fort St Elmo was the only building standing on the entire peninsula. Grand Master Jean Parisot de la Valette commissioned the construction of this uniform grid city as a symbol of victory. Money

Prime Minister and the President. Except for the architectural gem that is the Parliament building, no modern structures spoil the cityscape.

★ *Republic Street* is the main shopping street in Valletta, a lively pedestrian zone that cuts like a knife straight down the middle of the peninsula and is often decorated with flags and banners. The street is a popular venue for all kinds of events, from religious processions with brass bands, to carnival parades, fashion shows and anti-abortion demonstrations featuring bagpipe-playing boy scouts. You'll hear orchestras practising through open doorways and see street artists earning money from passers-by.

Valletta's charm lies in its diversity. Despite its historic towering buildings and narrow alleyways, you do not feel trapped inside the city's medieval walls. Its impressive, park-like bastions offer magnificent views out over the island, its bays and the wide-open sea between Africa and Europe.

SIGHTSEEING

1 FREEDOM SQUARE

The splendid renovation of Freedom Square in 2017 was an architectural gamble that paid off. It is the creation of Italian star architect Renzo Piano, who also designed Europe's highest skyscraper, the Shard in London, along with the Nemo in Amsterdam and the Paul Klee Centre in Bern. Here, in Valletta, Renzo Piano brought Malta's history to life. The old city gate was pulled down to open up views to the sky from this gently inclining square. Visitors can now access the once impenetrable fortification walls via a new wide open staircase.

Built completely from Gozitan limestone, the *Parliament Building* dominates the square. Renzo Piano's respect for nature was clear in the building process: the stone slabs were numbered as they were quarried and

then used in the same formation in the building as they had lain in the Maltese earth. The building symbolises a strong democracy: its seemingly windowless façade gives an imposing, bastion-like feel to the structure. Move closer, however, and you will notice that there are many large windows. The interior is only open to the public for a few days in the year, but all parliamentary debates are broadcast live on Parliament TV. The building is divided into two blocks connected via slender bridges on two levels. The blocks have been kept separate so as not to obscure views of the historic *St James Cavalier* – one of Malta's cultural strongholds. Visitors can walk between both parts of the building without going through any security checks, and get a privileged glimpse behind the scenes. Renzo Piano is also responsible for the striking *open-air theatre* next door: bombed during World War II, the ruins of the Royal Opera House have been cleverly converted to stand as a monument against war. *Valletta |* ⌘ *c4*

INSIDER TIP
Unexpected insight

2 NATIONAL MUSEUM OF ARCHAEOLOGY/AUBERGE DE PROVENCE ★

You won't have time to get bored in this museum! Built in 1574 for the Knights from Provence, this palace now houses an extremely modest collection of artefacts. Half an hour is all you need to understand why the Maltese were regarded as the most ingenious builders in Europe 5,000 years ago. Relying on the brute strength of man and animal, they built impressive buildings without the use of metal tools. If you want to learn more, there are audio guides available free of charge at the counter. Otherwise, just be amazed at how they managed to transport stone slabs weighing several tons across the island on stone rollers and lift them up to erect horizontal roofs. Other items include the oldest animal heads crafted by man (5000 BCE), the earliest local representations of the human figure (4400 BCE) and some splendid animal reliefs depicting a procession of five goats, a fish and a pig, with 22 other goats lined up two by two. Don't miss the temple models, which will give you a bird's-eye view of the structures before you encounter them up-close on a trip around the islands. The 5,000-year-old terracotta figure of a recumbent woman, known as the *Sleeping Lady* is one of the finest works of art from the Neolithic period. If you have developed a taste for archaeology during your visit, head up to the second floor to see other findings from the Bronze Age and Phoenician era. *Jan/Feb daily 9am–5pm, March–Dec daily 9am–6pm | admission 5 euros | Republic Street | Valletta | ⏱ 45 mins | ▥ c4*.

🔳 ST JOHN'S CO-CATHEDRAL ⭐

You won't find another church like this one! Even if you don't like churches, you should go and see it. The most unusual feature is the floor of the church. It is completely covered with 375 tombstones with inlay work in different colours of marble, beneath which Knights of St John are buried. The slabs bear inscriptions, coats of arms and many depictions of skulls and skeletons.

The walls and the ceiling are almost as impressive. Every little spot is ornamented. The chapels in the two aisles are each allocated to one of the *langues* of the Order, each one wanting to surpass the others in elegance and effort. On the left (from back to front) are the chapels of Germany, Italy, France, Provence and, finally, the joint chapel of Bavaria and Britain; on the right are those of Portugal and Castile, Aragón and the Auvergne.

The altarpiece of 1608 – Malta's most important painting – is the work of the Italian artist Michelangelo da Caravaggio. Today it hangs in the *oratory*. He depicted the dramatic beheading of John the Baptist with ingenious contrasts of light and shade. On the left, the young Salome holds a golden bowl to receive the head of John. In a macabre touch, Caravaggio signed his work in a pool of blood on the floor with the letters "fr. michelang".

Adjoining St John's Co-Cathedral is a *museum*, which is accessed from the oratory. It possesses 29 Gobelin tapestries made in Brussels in the 17th century. Each year in June they are hung in the cathedral. Fourteen of them depict scenes from the life of Christ, fourteen are allegories of the Catholic church, and one shows the Spanish Grand Master Perellos as the noble donor. *Co-Cathedral and Museum Mon–Fri 9.30am–4.30pm, Sat 9.30am–12.30pm | admission 10 euros | visitors' entrance on Republic*

*Street | Valletta | stjohnscocathedral.
com | ⏱ 1 hr | 🗺 d4.*

4 GRAND MASTER'S PALACE ★

Situated at the heart of Valletta, the palace is by no means a lifeless monument. Guards in parade uniforms stand in front of the main portal symbolically guarding the Maltese Prime Minister, whose office is housed here.

The austere two-storey façade is typical of the architectural style of the 16th century. The wooden corner bays are more recent, and the Baroque gateways were not added until the 18th century.

The wings of the Grand Master's Palace are grouped around two substantial inner courtyards, which are unexpectedly attractive: *Neptune*

Glittering St John's Co-Cathedral has an altarpiece by Caravaggio

Luxury limousines chauffeuring heads of state can often be seen driving past. The palace was the seat of the Parliament of Malta from 1963 to 2015. It was originally built as the palace of the Grand Master when the Order of St John established the new city of Valletta.

Court has a statue of the ancient god of the sea and a fountain that once served as a drinking trough for horses; *Prince Alfred's Court* has a slender palm tree and a lovely Andean pine. On the clock tower of this courtyard, bronze figures in Turkish uniforms have been striking the hour since 1745.

The *Armoury* is entered from Neptune Court. Here, many of the 5,700 weapons and items of armour that have survived from the time of the Knights of St John are on display, including the gilded armour of Grand Master Alof de Wignacourt (1601–22).

of St John and Knights Templar into battle in 1229.

In the *Ambassador's Room,* eight further frescoes record the history of the Order. The scenes represented here include the arrival of the knights on Rhodes in 1309 and their depar-

Admire the knights' suits of armour in the Armoury Corridor of the Grand Master's Palace

In the *State Rooms* on the upper floor, you first pass through the 31-m / 102-ft long *Palace Corridor* with ceiling paintings depicting the knights' naval battles and sea expeditions. In the *Yellow Room,* frescoes tell the story of the early years of the Order. Here, for example, you can see how the knights released King Louis IX of France from captivity at the hands of the Sultan of Egypt in 1250, or how King Frederick II led a company consisting of Knights

ture from there in 1522. Pope John XXIII, George Bush and Mikhail Gorbachev have all sat on the armchairs in this room. In the *Hall of the Supreme Council,* 12 frescoes are devoted to the Great Siege of 1565. Finally, in the *State Dining Room,* portraits of all presidents of Malta to date line the walls, alongside Queen Elizabeth II, who remained the official head of state of the island republic after its independence until 1974.

No one should leave the Grand Master's Palace without taking a look in the *Tapestry Chamber*. Until 1976, it was used as the chamber of the Maltese parliament. Ten unique Gobelin tapestries of silk and cotton hang on the walls. In glowing colours, they depict plants, landscapes, animals and people. They were woven around the year 1700 in the royal tapestry works of Louis XIV, the Manufacture Royale des Gobelins in Paris. The frescoes above the tapestries show the sea expeditions of the Knights of St John. *Armoury daily 9am–5pm, State Rooms Mon–Fri 10am–4.30pm, Sat/Sun 9am–4.30pm | joint ticket 10 euros | when the State Rooms are closed for official receptions, a special price for the Armoury alone applies: 6 euros | access via Republic Street | Valletta |* ⏱ *1 hr |* ⌖ *d4*

5 STRAIT STREET

Until the withdrawal of the British forces in 1963, Strait Street was the capital's notorious red light district. The last brothels then closed down and the street was left abandoned. Recently, new businesses have been attracted to this narrow street and its surroundings, making it a popular spot on Valletta's nightlife scene. *Valletta |* ⌖ *d3*

6 MANOEL THEATRE

No matter where you are in the world, you can reserve, pay for and even print out tickets online in a matter of minutes to guarantee front-row seats in one of the world's oldest continually running theatres, built in 1732.

It is worth visiting the opulent oval auditorium, which seats a total of 600 spectators, even when there is no performance. It has four tiers of boxes that are made entirely from painted wood. Adjoining the theatre are a theatre museum and an upscale souvenir shop. *Guided tours Mon–Fri 9.30am–4.30pm, Sat 9.30am–12.30pm every 45 mins | 5 euros | Old Theatre Street | Valletta | teatrumanoel.com.mt |* ⌖ *d3*

7 CASA ROCCA PICCOLA

Although you wouldn't necessarily choose to live among the overwhelming number of valuable antiques housed in this 16th-century palazzo, a visit provides a unique insight into the privileged lifestyle of the Maltese aristocracy, in this case the ninth Marquis de Piro and his family. Opened in 2017 by the marquis's son, Clement, a small number of carefully restored guestrooms are now available for rent within the splendid palazzo. If you want to be fairly sure that your tour guide is a member of the aristocratic family, then book the Champagne Tour. *(Fri 7pm | 25 euros | booking essential).* However, all the young staff members (each of whom is profiled on the website) are also thoroughly engaging and have plenty of anecdotes to recount. Those interested in delving into the palace's history should go down into the World War II air-raid shelters, where the Piro family sought refuge from German and Italian bombs. *Mon–Sat 10am–4pm hourly | admission 9 euros | 74 Republic*

INSIDER TIP
Nobility bonus

Street | Valletta | casarocapiccola.com |
⊙ 45 mins | ▥ e3

8 FORT ST ELMO

Standing on the fort, you can almost hear the sounds of war reverberating from the walls. When the Turks invaded the island in 1565, the fort occupied a solitary position on the uninhabited peninsula, now the site of Valletta. The fort bore the brunt of the Turkish attack, and the decapitated heads of captured warriors were fired from here in retaliation. In World War II, the British used the fort as a last defence to prevent the German and Italian boats and submarines from invading the Grand Harbour. The *National War Museum (April–Sept daily 9am–6pm, Oct–March daily 9am–5pm | admission 10 euros)* inside the fort focuses more on the bravery than the suffering of the soldiers and the civilian population, with part of the exhibition showing off military tactics and techniques.

Every Sunday, more than 50 men dress up in colourful uniforms with authentic weapons to perform full-scale military drills for the *In-Guardia Parade (Sun 11–11.45am | dates at visitmalta.com)*, a testament to the glory rather than the atrocities of war.
⊙ 1–1.5 hrs | ▥ f2

9 MALTA EXPERIENCE / SACRA INFERMIA 🛏 ★

A noisy and colourful sprint through Malta's history is provided by this audiovisual show – the best of many on offer on the island: *Malta Experience (Mon–Fri 11am–4pm*

hourly, Sat–Sun 11am, noon and 1pm, also 2pm Oct–June | admission 16 euros | themaltaexperience.com). The 45-minute show incorporates 3,000 images that are accompanied by impressive quadraphonic sound effects, with explanations provided via headsets in 14 languages, one on every channel. Afterwards, you'll be in know doubt what to see during your holiday on Malta.

The show's venue is the courtyard of the spacious hospital built by the Knights of St John in 1575. The *Sacra Infermeria* was the most modern hospital of its day. Every patient had his or her own bed, a luxury which few would have had at home. In total, there were over 1,000 beds in six different wards. Medical care was carried out by doctors and nurses who were trained by the Order itself. The food was served on silver plates for hygienic reasons. Even knights from aristocratic families had to regularly work in a humble capacity treating sick persons who were often far below them in social status. Religious belief or prisoner-of-war status did not affect the rights of a patient to receive care: there was even a small ward for Muslims who had been captured.

The largest of the wards is 160m / 525ft long, and is now often used as an events venue; at other times it can be visited on the same ticket as the *Malta Experience Show*. The cellar vaults house another exhibition entitled *The Knights Hospitallers (9.30am–4.30pm | admission 5 euros)* which provides an insight into the knights' highly progressive hospital system using original items, models and recreated scenes. *St Lazarus Bastion | Triq Il-Mediterran | Valletta |* ⏱ *1 hr |* 🗺 *f3*

🔟 LOWER BARRACCA GARDENS

Soak up Valletta's maritime past and present in this small park. Built to commemorate Malta's first British High Commissioner, the garden's Doric temple nestles in a sea of flowers with views of the Grand Harbour below where you can watch real-life sailors at work: pilots boarding freight and cruise ships, tugs towing these giant liners out to sea and captains trying to manoeuvre their vessels in and out of the narrow harbour. *Free access | Triq Mediterran | Valletta |* 🗺 *e–f4*

🔟 CRUISE TERMINAL

There are usually at least two or three ships docked at the cruise terminal on the Grand Harbour. These luxury liners are the stuff of holiday dreams. Although you are forbidden to go on board without a reservation, you can get a great view of the ships from one of the many nice cafés and restaurants on the *Valletta Waterfront*. 🗺 *c6*

🔟 UPPER BARRACCA GARDENS/ SALUTING BATTERY 🚩

Valletta's most beautiful park, laid out back in 1775 on the *Bastion of St Peter and Paul*, occupies the highest point on the city wall and affords a magnificent view of the Grand Harbour and the old towns of Senglea and Vittoriosa, and of the shipyards and

The Siege Bell War Memorial affords great views of shipping in the Grand Harbour

INSIDER TIP
You and Sir Winston

the lower-lying parts of the capital.

Do you fancy a selfie with Britain's wartime Prime Minister? You'll find a statue of Sir Winston Churchill in the park. There's also a fine sculpture of three street children by the Maltese artist Antonio Sciortino. *Castille Square | Valletta.*

The terrace directly below the park is the 🚩 *Saluting Battery (daily 10am–5pm, gun salute at noon and at 4pm | admission 3 euros | access from Upper Barracca Gardens and Battery Street | salutingbattery.com).* Just as in British colonial times, a cannon is fired here at exactly noon and again at 4pm. It's so punctual that you can set your watch by it. In fact, in colonial times the gun salute at high noon was used to set the official time for all ships' clocks in order to aid their navigation at sea. *▢ d5*

🔟 LASCARIS WAR ROOMS

The memories of war are ever-present in Valletta, but this underground bunker, located beneath a bastion built by the Knights of John, is particularly significant, not only for Malta but for the course of world history. The room was used by General Dwight D. Eisenhower to direct the allied invasion of Sicily. The atmosphere of tension that prevailed here is still palpable, and even the maps of the operation are still intact. The invasion began on 10 July 1943, and ended with the deposition of the Italian dictator Mussolini on 24 July. *Daily 10am–5pm | admission 12 euros |*

entrance via Battery Street next to the Upper Barracca Gardens or from Lascaris Ditch | Valletta | wirtartna.org | ⏱ 40–50 mins | ▢ d5.

🔢 MUZA ☂

Malta's newest museum showcases the country's contemporary art scene in the former palace of the Italian knights, the Auberge d'Italie. In the inner courtyard, the museum café serves as a public meeting point where Maltese art is at the forefront of the conversation. Amateur contemporary artists share the walls with esteemed local artists from the last 200 years. *Daily 9am–5pm, Courtyard café 8am–10pm | Merchants Street |*

Apart from the daily gun salute, the Upper Barracca Gardens are a tranquil spot

Valletta | muza.heritagemalta.org | ⏱ 30–50 mins | 🗺 d4

🕴 AUBERGE DE CASTILLE, LÉON E PORTUGAL

When the red carpet is rolled out, it signals the arrival of a high-ranking guest. The 18th-century palace of the Knights of the Iberian Peninsula, known as the Auberge de Castille, Léon e Portugal, is now the impressive seat of Malta's Prime Minister. The official state car, currently an Alfa Romeo without registration plate, is often parked right outside – not something that would be possible outside 10 Downing Street. *Closed to visitors | Castille Place | Valletta | 🗺 c5*

🕴 ST JAMES CAVALIER

Art instead of war. The fort of St James, once a formidable but unremarkable bulwark on the landward side of the city walls, has been converted into a lively *Centre for Creativity*. It's the location for concerts and for changing exhibitions showcasing contemporary Maltese arts and crafts. Equally atmospheric are the small theatre, where you're close to the action on stage, and the arthouse cinema, which screens engaging but challenging films. *Daily 10am–9pm | programme information: tel. 21 22 32 00 or kreattivita.org | free admission | Pope Pius V Street | Valletta | 🗺 c5*

> **INSIDER TIP**
> **An evening of culture**

🔟 SLIEMA FERRY

The lively hub of Sliema is an interchange for buses and the boarding point for boat trips around the harbour and for ferries over to Valletta. The cafés and fast-food restaurants are especially popular as hangouts for international language students and their teachers. *Sliema* | 🗺 *M8*

around the bay. Sit on one of the restaurant and bar terraces overlooking the water, on the *pjazza* beneath the Judas trees or outside the Labour Party offices, *band club* and McDonald's to watch the world go by.

There's a great view of the Valletta skyline from Sliema

🔟 BALLUTA BAY

One of the most photogenic spots on the entire island. In summer, hundreds of brightly coloured boats squeeze into this narrow harbour while Malta's nightlife pulsates all

Love is the title of the prominently placed modern sculpture by Richard England, an internationally acclaimed Maltese architect, poet and artist. Why are the letters deliberately turned upside down? So they can be read when they are reflected in the water. Love does indeed move in mysterious ways. *Promenade between Sliema and St Julian's* | 🗺 *M7*

EATING & DRINKING

ANGELICA

According to celebrity chef, restaurateur and food connoisseur, Jamie Oliver, this restaurant serves the best

rabbit dish in Malta. We would not argue with him, although the calamari filled with smoked fish and salmon are equally good. Fans of Greek food who want to try something a little different will find a Maltese-style moussaka on the dinner menu, alongside many other specialities depending on the season and the ingredients available. The establishment is tiny so make sure you book in advance. *Daily | 134 Archbishop Street | Valletta | tel. 21 22 27 77 | €€ | ⅏ e4*

AVENUE

The most popular place in Paceville, a 340-seater restaurant that is always full. Light wood, a lot of colour, big portions, good value for money. Pizza, pasta, burgers and salads, grill dishes. Not for gourmets, but the right atmosphere for dinner before a night out. *Daily, Sun evening only | corner of Gort Street / Paceville Street | Paceville | tel. 21 31 17 53 | € | ⅏ M7*

BLUE ROOM

Forget red and golden dragons and paper lanterns, this is a different kind of Chinese restaurant. Seating just 40 guests, this eatery offers a modern interior, low-fat food, modest menu and contemporary dishes: duck breast in Chinese pancakes to be eaten with chopsticks. *Daily, Sat evening only | 59 Republic Street | Valletta | tel. 21 23 80 14 | €€ | ⅏ d3*

HENRY J. BEANS

The laid-back eatery in the *Corinthia St George* hotel complex is a favourite meeting place for young Maltese in the 20–35 age group. Everything is American here, from the decor and the music to the food: hamburgers, spare ribs, steaks and fajitas are top choices. Theme parties with live music take place at weekends. *Daily from noon, Happy Hour 5.30–7pm | St George's Bay | St Julian's | tel. 21 37 90 16 55 | €€ | ⅏ M7*

Republic Street is traffic-free – ideal for stress-free shopping

IS SUQ TAL-BELT

Valletta's historic 19th-century market hall is now the city's food market. Buy food from all over the world at the numerous stalls and then consume it with everyone else at the communal tables. Whether you fancy tapas or sushi, pasta, pizza or burgers, kebabs, pulled pork or something Maltese, you'll find it here. There's even a mozzarella bar serving 14 varieties of the cheese and a stand that only sells cake and dessert. *Daily 7am–1am | Merchants Street | Valletta | € |* 🕮 *d–e4*

INSIDER TIP
Naughty but nice

LEGLIGIN

You'll need to be a little bit adventurous to enjoy this local restaurant. It's accessed via a couple of steps down to a cellar and, once inside, there's not even a menu. Chef Cyrille Darras cooks whatever she feels like; then her staff serve it to the customers. There may be six, seven or even eight courses to try, offering a cross-section of Maltese cuisine refined with French touches. The evening menu costs under 30 euros; at lunchtime, it's just 20 euros, and allergies and other special requests are all taken into account. Many Maltese wines are available by the glass, which means you can choose a suitable one to go with each course. *Daily | 117–119 Santa Lucia Street | Valletta | €€ | ⊞ c3*

LE MALTE

Traditional Maltese food for ordinary guests. This small business is run by a friendly family and serves moderately priced dishes. The set menu is particularly recommended: three courses, including wine and coffee, with rabbit or bragioli roulade as a main dish. *Daily, Mon–Thu evenings only | 139c Tower Road | Sliema | tel. 99 87 86 99 | € | ⊞ M7*

LA MALTIJA

Maltese dining for celebrities. Joint proprietor and chef Charles Spiteri has received a TV award as Malta's best cook, and has had the honour of cooking for Maltese presidents and international dignitaries. The fresh fish and seafood, from oysters to langoustines, are especially recommended. Booking essential. *Mon–Sat dinner only | 1 Church Street | Paceville | tel. 21 35 96 02 | www.lamaltija. com | €€ | ⊞ M7*

PEPPINO'S

Classic Italian on three floors, with a roof terrace and smokers' room. The lamb dishes are good. *Mon–Sat | 31 St George's Road | St Julian's | tel. 21 37 32 00 | €€€ | ⊞ M7*

VECCHIA NAPOLI

A proper Italian. Naples, Ischia and Campania influences prevail in the kitchen of this restaurant, well-known all over the island for its pizzas. Service is friendly and efficient. *Daily for dinner, Sat/Sun also lunch | 255 Tower Road | Sliema | tel. 21 34 34 24 | €–€€ | ⊞ M7*

SHOPPING

The good thing about shopping in Valletta is that there aren't any boring chains or department stores; most shops are independently owned and managed. They are clustered around ★ *Republic Street* and its side streets in the old town. This is the number one shopping destination on Malta. It is also worth taking a look at the shops along *Merchants Street*, where the revamped former market hall *Is-Suq Tal-Belt (Mon–Sat 7am–2pm)* has been been attracting customers with its winning combination of shopping and dining since 2018.

AGENDA

The best bookshop on the island with a wide range of coffee-table books and lots of literature about Malta and Gozo in numerous languages. *26 Republic Street | Valletta | millermalta.com | ⊞ c4*

ANTHONY D'AMATO

If you're looking for an old favourite on vinyl, this place will either already have it in stock, or they'll track it down for you, as long as it still exists. The d'Amato family has been in the music business since 1885, and their shop looks as though it is nearly as old. The Maltese songs they issued on their own label are only

INSIDER TIP
Vinyl detective

available on *Malta. 99 St John Street | Valletta | ⊞ d4*

THE POINT 👕

The Maltese are not behind the times when it comes to fashion; they know how to appreciate international labels, and all the high-end brands and names in fashion can be found on the three floors of Malta's newest shopping mall. It doesn't replace a shopping trip to London, Paris or New York, but it weighs on your wallet just the same. *Mon–Sat 9.30am–7.30pm | Tigne Point | Sliema ⊞ M8*

THE SILVERSMITH'S SHOP 🚩

Silversmith Maurice Borg is a real gem and loves to chat. Good conversation starters are provided by the postcards from all over the world that line the walls of his workshop. They've been sent to him by customers who have been charmed by lively conversations with this friendly silversmith. He is also happy to discuss his fine filigree silverwork, sold at extremely reasonably prices – not much more than a burger. *218 Republic Street | Valletta | ⊞ e3*

WEMBLEY STORE

Don't visit this gourmet food emporium on an empty stomach. Behind its trademark green timber façade, this three-floor shop sells the finest foods and wines from Malta, Italy and around the world. It's a good place to stock up on snacks for a day exploring the city. There's also plenty on offer for vegans and those with special dietary requirements. Italian craft beer is sold

Not a grain of sand in sight among the flat rocks near Sliema

in original bottles, and Maltese pastries are freshly filled for each customer. *Mon–Sat all day, Sun 10am–1pm | 305 Republic Street | Valletta | ᗊ c4*

BEACHES & POOLS

You don't need a beach for a spot of sunbathing. Watch the Maltese locals to see how it's done. Simply spread out your towel or mat on the broad cliffs and set up your camping furniture and BBQ by the sea – it doesn't cost a penny. If you don't mind paying for your creature comforts, head instead to Sliema for its diverse selection of beach clubs and pool terraces. Even some of the hotels have access to private beach pools. If you plan to swim in the sea, use the ladders provided and wear swim shoes.

NEPTUNE'S FRESHWATER POOL ✯

This big freshwater pool with its own paddling pool is cheap and therefore popular with students and language-school pupils. There's a restaurant, a bar and a diving school on site. *Day ticket 5–10 euros depending on the season, 50% discount for students after 4pm | Balluta Bay | St Julian's | neptuneswpsc.com | ᗊ M7*

PARADISE EXILES

This simple beach bar, with an old-fashioned jukebox instead of a modern DJ console, rents out loungers and parasols on the rocks at the south end of Balluta Bay. The atmosphere on the bar terrace is very laid-back during the summer. Come here to chill out. *Parasol 5 euros | Balluta Bay | Sliema | ᗊ M7*

SLIEMA PITCH

The biggest of the seawater pools, right by the sea, is owned by the water polo club of Sliema, which has over 2,500 members. To accommodate them all, there is a large restaurant, which is especially popular for Sunday lunch. Swimmers enter the sea via ladders; parasols are available for hire. *Day ticket 10 euros | Tower Road | near Fortizza | Sliema | sliema-asc.org.mt | ⊞ M7*

SPORT & ACTIVITIES

CHALLENGER GYM

If you don't want to give up your fitness training while you're on holiday, you can train with the locals at this gym in the centre of town. *Mon–Fri 8am–10pm, Sat 8am–4pm, Sun 8am– noon | 7 euros per day, 20 euros per week | Zachary Street | Valletta | tel. 21 44 31 01 | challengemalta.com | ⊞ c–d4*

EDEN SUPER BOWL

There are 20 lanes at your disposal at this bowling alley, which also hosts national league games and international tournaments. *St Augustine Road | Paceville | tel. 21 38 73 98 | edensuperbowl.com | ⊞ M7*

NIGHTLIFE

Boredom is not an issue here. The promenade between Valletta and Paceville is always a hive of activity in the evenings, with newly opened bars and lounges appearing all the time. Most of the clientele are over 30; they

appreciate stylish surroundings and quieter spaces.

Not so in St Julian's and especially in Paceville (pronounced Pah-tshe-vill), which has earned itself a reputation as the mega party lounge of the central Mediterranean. In summer, and all year round at weekends, the partying spills out from the bars, clubs and discos onto the streets, which are mostly traffic-free. Here the under-18s, who are not admitted to clubs, can join in the fun. Entry to most clubs and discos is free.

ALCHEMY

In the old days, alchemists sought to create gold. In this tiny bar, you'll find passionate mixologist Attila Felhosi and his team mixing gold-standard signature cocktails instead, using secret ingredients. The atmosphere is magical. *Daily from 2pm | 93–94 Strait Street | Valletta | alchemyvalletta.com | ⊞ d3*

INSIDER TIP
In seventh cocktail heaven

BLACKBULL PUB

This pub at the heart of the entertainment district is a central hang-out between dance venues. Chill out here on the street before clubbing starts or in between. *Daily | Dragonara Road | Paceville | tel. 21 37 13 63 | ⊞ M7*

BRIDGE BAR

Are you in a romantic mood, ready for a harbour view and some good music? The bar in the house with the red bay windows is much too small to accommodate everyone, so romantics also sit at tables on the bridge by Victoria Gate or make use of the cushions that are strewn on the steps. Wine, beer and either street food or first-class cheese platters are served every evening, and on Fridays from May to October there's jazz on the menu too. *Daily | East Street | Valletta | ⌑ d5*

CAFÉ SOCIETY

Good cocktails and long drinks at fair prices are enough of a draw for many of the Maltese regulars. Another attraction is the harbour view from the few tables scattered in the street outside. Most important, however, are the live performances by solo musicians and bands. Jazz and funk are the dominant sounds, and many of the performers are members of the Malta Sound Women Network which is supported by the café. *Daily 5.30pm– 1am | 13 St John's Street | Valletta | cafesocietyvalletta.com | ⌑ d4–5*

CASEY'S BAR

This small bar in a residential area is a real social hub. The open-mic nights on Tuesdays and Saturdays are open to everyone: musicians, comics and poets can all take to the stage; there's even an electric guitar on hand. On Fridays, local bands are invited to play, while on Mondays less talented performers can practise their karaoke skills. *Daily from 6pm | 306 D'Argens Street | Gira | ⌑ M8*

Paceville: where young partygoers keep the night alive

Nightclubs, discos and bars jostle for custom in Paceville

CASINO DRAGONARA PALACE

Malta's oldest casino is situated at the tip of a rocky promontory near the Westin Dragonara Hotel in Paceville. Roulette, stud poker, blackjack and punto blanco are all on offer, and 170 one-armed bandits are on hand to suck up any left-over change. For Maltese, the minimum age is 25; for others, 18. An ID card is needed for admission, but men need not wear a tie. Refreshments are available from the bar and restaurant *(daily | €€€)*. *Daily | Paceville | tel. 21 38 23 62 | dragonara.com | ⫼ M7*

CHARLES GRECH

Each to their own! Situated directly on Republic Street, this art deco bar with outdoor seating sets no boundaries. While one guest orders a glass of hot milk for 1.20 euros, the other splashes out on wine for 1,600 euros a bottle. Some come for a relaxing drink after a full day's shopping; others turn up dressed to the nines. The drinks menu includes 73 different types of whiskey, and the most expensive champagne costs around the same as a small car. Candle-lit tables and formally dressed waiters complete the look of this long-standing establishment. You can choose your own Havana cigar from the walk-through underground humidor; it also stocks a selection of Maltese delicacies to take away. *Closed Sun | 10 Republic Street | Valletta | ⫼ c4*

INSIDER TIP
Champagne and cigars

EDEN CENTURY CINEMA COMPLEX ☂

The latest releases and classic films are shown in the original English or Italian versions. The complex holds 16 modern screens and the Mediterranean's first Imax Vodafone Film Centre. *St Augustine Road | Paceville | reservations tel. 21 37 64 01 | programme tel. 21 37 64 04 | edencinemas.com.mt | ⚏ M7*

GUY'S BAR PLOUGH & ANCHOR RESTAURANT

One of Malta's most authentic pubs is English all over. The landlord collects beer mugs decorated with the faces of famous figures from politics and show-business. Play 'Who's who?' with your friends and see how many of them you can identify. Among over 400 kinds of spirits, there are lots of malt whiskies to choose from. *Closed Mon | 263 Tower Road | Sliema | tel. 21 33 47 25 | ⚏ M7*

INSIDER TIP
Jug heads

HARD ROCK CAFE

This Maltese outpost of the global chain retains its usual, ubiquitous style – with an original guitar from Brian May of Queen as a showpiece. *Daily | Level 2 | Bay Street Centre | Paceville | hardrock.com | ⚏ M7*

HAVANA 🐷

Giant club with six bars on two floors, accommodating 3,000. The three dancing zones have different styles of music: music of black origin, best of commercial and best of the '60s–'90s. *Daily | St George's Road | Paceville | tel. 21 37 45 00 | ⚏ M7*

MONALIZA VALLETTA

A lounge bar with an international outlook. This place celebrates the diversity of global cultures, with quotes on its homepage from Steve Jobs, Nelson Mandela and Martin Luther King, among others. The finest cocktails, long drinks, beers and wines are served at extremely moderate prices, alongside various food platters for up to eight people – and the music is just as multicultural as the staff working here. The venue hosts fashion shows, and there's dancing on occasion, too. *Daily | 222 Great Siege Road | Valletta | tel. 77 38 23 03 | monaliza.com.mt | ⚏ b3*

SHADOW LOUNGE

VIP treatment at moderate prices. The dress code is formal at Hugo's Shadow Lounge. Golden sofas, glass and metallic furnishings are in keeping with the tastes of its clientele who order vodka in 4.5-litre bottles. The lounge bar caters to others though, with a bottle of beer costing less than 3 euros and a glass of prosecco for around the same. Although there's capacity for 500 guests, it is essential to book a table. Top Maltese DJs create the right vibe in this self-styled "high octane nightclub". *Fri/Sat | St George's Road | Paceville | shadowloungemalta. com | ⚏ M7*

AROUND VALLETTA

HYPOGEUM ★

6km (3.7 miles) / approx.15 mins by bus from the main terminal in Valletta

A unique and amazing sight: built 5,000 years ago, this subterranean necropolis has survived the passage of time with little damage. There is nothing quite like it anywhere else in the world. You should book well in advance as the number of daily visitors is restricted. On an area of 500m² | 5,382 sq ft, three storeys have been hewn out of the rock to a depth of 14m / 46ft. Here you will see passages and halls, chambers, niches and steps, as well as the remains of wall paintings that mainly consist of decorative motifs such as tendrils and spirals. Many of the features are similar to those in the Neolithic temples above ground. For example, there are oracle holes and even a hole for tying up sacrificial animals.

The Hypogeum was discovered by chance in 1902 during excavation work for a rainwater cistern. The archaeologists who were called in to excavate this underground labyrinth found about 7,000 complete skeletons and the remains of 20,000 more, which suggests it was a burial site. Some researchers believe that these subterranean chambers were also a place of initiation for priestesses who served the great mother goddess, the Magna Mater, in temples.

Hypogeum in Paola: was this subterranean labyrinth once an initiation site for priestesses?

Statuettes of two sleeping women have been found in the Hypogeum, including the famous *Sleeping Lady*, which is now on display in the *National Museum of Archaeology* in Valletta (see p. 45). Did the priestesses spend time in the Hypogeum in this way so that the spirit of the deity could enter them while they were asleep?

A maximum of 70 visitors per day are allowed onto the site in groups of ten. First they watch a short introductory video and then follow a prescribed 20-minute route through this fascinating subterranean world.

AROUND VALLETTA

INSIDER TIP
The early bird catches the worm

Buy your tickets for admission before you leave home, otherwise you've no chance of getting in. *Tickets (approx. 35 euros) for the daily tours at 9am, 10am, 11am, 1pm, 2pm and 3pm can be purchased in advance at heritagemalta.org and at the ticket desks of all museums and archaeological sites managed by Heritage Malta; tickets (40 euros) for the daily tours at noon and 4pm are only available on the previous day from the ticket desks at Fort St Elmo in Valletta on Malta and at the archaeological museums in Victoria on Gozo | entrance Triq ic-Cimiterju | Paola | ▥ M9*

TARXIEN ★

7km (4.3 miles) / approx. 15 mins by bus from the main bus terminal in Valletta

In a modern built-up area of the town of Tarxien lie the impressive remains of the largest Maltese temple complex. It consists of four separate temples that were constructed between 3800 and 2500 BCE; three of them are well preserved and have even been partly rebuilt.

In 2016, a giant protective cover resembling a giant butterfly was erected over the temples. A series of raised walkways leads you around the complex, with opportunities to see inside the temples at certain points. The explanatory panels and the information provided in the adjoining visitor centre will give you a clear impression of the workings of this former cult site. *Daily 9am–5pm | admission 6 euros | Neolithic Temple Street | Tarxien | ▥ M9*

Classic sailing boats moor alongside super-yachts on Vittoriosa's waterfront

VITTORIOSA (BIRGU)

(￫ N8) **So this is how gentle tourism can be!** ★ **Vittoriosa still does not attract masses of tourists, even though, after Valletta and Mdina, it is the most historically interesting town on the island. This makes it all the more attractive. You'd do well to spend an afternoon and an evening here.**

It is only towards Dockyard Creek that the old knights' town of Vittoriosa (population 3,000) opens itself to the modern world. Fifty-metre yachts moor at the quayside on *Vittoriosa*

Waterfront, and a few cafés and restaurants give you an opportunity to sit right by the water, especially in the evening. The exclusive *Grand Harbour Marina* was inaugurated in 2005 by the Queen in person.

Before the Knights of St John founded Valletta, they resided here in Vittoriosa, which was then called *Birgu*. Birgu, rather than Valletta, was the target of the Turkish siege in 1565. Today, Vittoriosa has nothing of the flavour of a capital city. Most of the residents are employed as stevedores or dock workers. Vittoriosa is a residential town with a largely southern Italian character and a scattering of historic monuments from the time of the Knights of St John.

Nearly all the surviving or reconstructed buildings from that time can only be viewed from the outside. One of the most impressive is the *Hospital of the Order* on Triq Il-Miratur. It was among the first buildings constructed by the Order and dates back to 1532. Additional buildings from the time of the knights, all of which are marked by marble plaques on the outer walls, can be found on Triq Hilda Tabone. These include the *Auberge de France* (no. 24/27), the *Auberge de Castille* (no. 57), the *Auberge de Portugal* (no. 59) and the *Auberge d'Auvergne et de Provence* (no. 17/23). In Triq Mistral stands the *Auberge d'Angleterre* (no. 39/40)

SIGHTSEEING

FORT ST ANGELO

On the very tip of the peninsula between Kalkara and Dockyard Creek stands Fort St Angelo, which was built by the knights before the Great Siege of 1565. The site was previously occupied by a Byzantine and then an Arab castle. Vittoriosa is defended on the landward side by a massive wall. *April–Sept daily 9am–6pm, Oct–March daily 9am–5pm | admission 8 euros | access from the end of Vittoriosa Waterfront | ⏱ 30 mins*

INQUISITOR'S PALACE 👹

Vittoriosa's most important building is the two-storey Inquisitor's Palace, which dates from 1535. Visitors can view the courtroom – into which the accused were led through a purposefully low doorway, so that they had to bow their heads humbly as they entered – the prison courtyard, the cells and the site of the gallows. Actors dressed in costume entertainingly re-enact interrogation and torture scenes. Until 1798, this was the seat of 62 inquisitors who were appointed by the pope; there is no record of the number of their victims. *Daily 9am–5pm | admission 6 euros | Triq Il-Palazz Ta' L-Isqof | ⏱ 1 hr*

MALTA AT WAR MUSEUM

Pass through the *Gate of Provence* to reach the main street, called Triq il-Mina L-Kbira. Here on the left, a sign points the way down to the Malta at War Museum. Exhibits from World War II and a 30-minute film about

Malta in the war are presented in tunnels hacked out of the rock. *Daily 10am–5pm | admission 10 euros | Couvre Port | wirtartna.org | ⊙ 1 hr*

SAN LAWRENZ/ ORATORJU SAN GUZEPP

Down on Dockyard Creek, the richly ornate façade of the baroque parish church opens onto the waterfront. In the oratory, among knightly belongings, is an icon from Rhodes.

Next to the church, near the quayside, the Freedom Monument commemorates the departure of the last British soldiers from Malta in 1979. *Triq San Lawrenz*

FOR PARTY ANIMALS

Valentina *(94 rooms | Schreiber Street | Paceville | tel. 21 38 22 32 | hotelvalentina.com | € | ⌂ M7)* is the place to stay if you never want to be far from Paceville's party scene. It's a practical solution. Ninety-four rooms are spread over five floors and each has its own iPod docking station. The rooms around the inner cour,tyard are the quietest.

FOR CITY ROMANTICS

Valletta Nobile *(3 double rooms | no children | Triq San Nikola | Valletta | tel. 79 48 80 47 | vallettanobile.com | €€ | ⌂ D5)* is a house from the era of the knights, full of antiques but also boasting up-to-date technology; there are wooden balconies and bay windows, but also microwaves, DVDs and iPods.

EATING & DRINKING

BEBIRGU

On the town's principal square, Misrah Ir-Rebha, this romantic café restaurant is housed in the stylish clubhouse belonging to the *Muzikali Banda Vittoriosana San Lawrenz* from 1883. There's a huge ancient billiard table in the courtyard of the clubhouse where you can practise your cue skills. *Daily | tel. 77 22 00 77 | Misrah Ir-Rebha | €*

> **INSIDER TIP**
> Snooker, poo or billiards

DON BERTO

This is one of six venues on the Vittoriosa waterfront with a view of yachts belonging to the wealthy and the beautiful. From the slow-food menu, the lamb tagliata for two is especially delicious, thanks to its four-hour marinade. Also recommended is the pork neck, which is slow-cooked for 24 hours. For a starter, try one of the interesting platters; choose from an Italian, a Maltese and a fish version. *Marina | tel. 21 80 80 08 | €€€ | ⌂ N8*

OSTERIA.VE

The "ve" in the name stands for "Veneto", the region around Venice whose cuisine is lovingly prepared in the kitchen here. The fish lasagne is as excellent as the lamb chops, and the atmosphere is authentically Italian. *Wed–Mon evening, Sat/Sun also afternoons | Pope Alessandru VII Street | osteriave.com | €€*

VITTORIOSA

Fort St Angelo

Xatt Juan B. Azopardo

Triq Marina

Triq ir-Rinella

Triq il-Ponta

Triq iż-Żewġ Mini

Ix-Xatt tal-Birgu

Triq San Lawrenz

Triq San Filippu

Triq Hilda Tabone

Triq il-Mandraġġ

Don Berto

BeBirgu

San Lawrenz/
Oratorju San Guzepp

Tal-Petut

Inquisitor's Palace

Triq is-Sur

Triq il-Vittorja

Triq San Guzepp

Triq Pawlu Boffa

Osteria.Ve

Triq ix-Xatt

200 m
219 yd

Malta at War Museum

Triq San Dwardu

TAL-PETUT

The proprietor, Don, prepares a Maltese menu that changes daily. You're advised to book by telephone at weekends. *Tue–Sat evenings | Triq Pacifiku Scicluna 20 | tel. 99 51 58 83 | €€*

AROUND VITTORIOSA

SENGLEA/ISLA

2km (1.25 miles) / 25 mins on foot or 5 mins by car from Vittoriosa

Are you looking for a coastal resort that isn't overrun with tourists? Then take bus line 2 to the end terminal in Senglea (pop. 3,500), known in the Maltese language as L-Isla. Many

locals – including dock workers – still live in this corner of Malta, which has not yet suffered at the hands of gentrification. Most tourists only manage to reach the *Vedette (freely accessible),* at the farthest tip of this peninsula, for a quick photo opportunity overlooking the town; this small lookout post, high above the Grand Harbour, has one of the very best views in urban Malta. The carvings of two eyes and two ears in low relief are intended to symbolise the alertness of the defenders of Malta.

From here, you can take a leisurely stroll around the end of Dockyard Creek to Vittoriosa. Take a break at one of the tables at the *Alice Springs kiosk (daily | €)* where crowds of locals gather for hot dogs and coffee for one euro. ▥ *M8*

SOUTHEAST MALTA

NOT JUST FOR THE TOURISTS

The villages and small towns in this region remain largely the preserve of the Maltese. While the authentic fishing village of Marsaxlokk, the Stone Age temple of Hagar Qim/Mnajdra and the Blue Grotto draw in droves of daytrippers, there are very few hotels and hardly any beaches to attract holidaymakers.

This is where you'll find out how Malta makes a living: the southeast is the largest industrial area on the island, location of both the electricity power station and the container port. The IT sector also has

Fishing boats in Marsaxlokk

its home here, in the new Smart City, while international screen stars make use of the film studios next door. The only space left for the untamed natural world is the south coast. This can be best experienced at the temples of Mnajdra and Hagar Qim, or by walking from there to Wiediz-Zurrieq, from where you can take a boat along the steep coastline to enjoy the magical lightshow in the Blue Grotto. In conclusion, the southeast deserves at least a day trip; independent travellers could choose to spend a couple of nights in one of the few small pensions in Marsaxlokk.

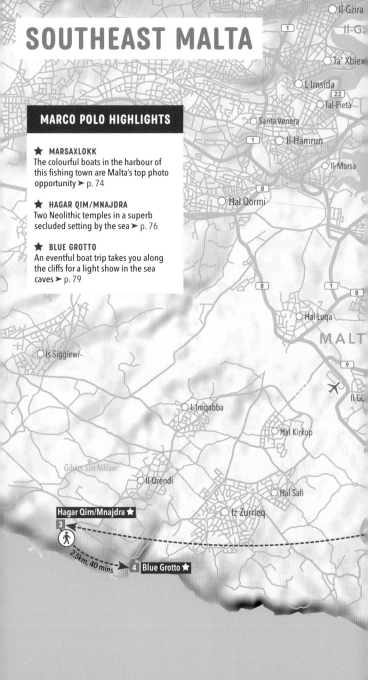

SOUTHEAST MALTA

MARCO POLO HIGHLIGHTS

★ **MARSAXLOKK**
The colourful boats in the harbour of this fishing town are Malta's top photo opportunity ➤ p. 74

★ **HAGAR QIM/MNAJDRA**
Two Neolithic temples in a superb secluded setting by the sea ➤ p. 76

★ **BLUE GROTTO**
An eventful boat trip takes you along the cliffs for a light show in the sea caves ➤ p. 79

Il-Gżira
Ta' Xbiex
L-Imsida
Tal-Pietà
Santa Venera
Il-Hamrun
Il-Marsa
Hal Qormi
MALT
Hal Luqa
Il-G
Is-Siġġiewi
L-Imqabba
Hal Kirkop
Gibjun San Niklaw
Il-Qrendi
Hal Safi
Iż-Żurrieq

Hagar Qim/Mnajdra ★
3
2.5km, 40 mins
4 Blue Grotto ★

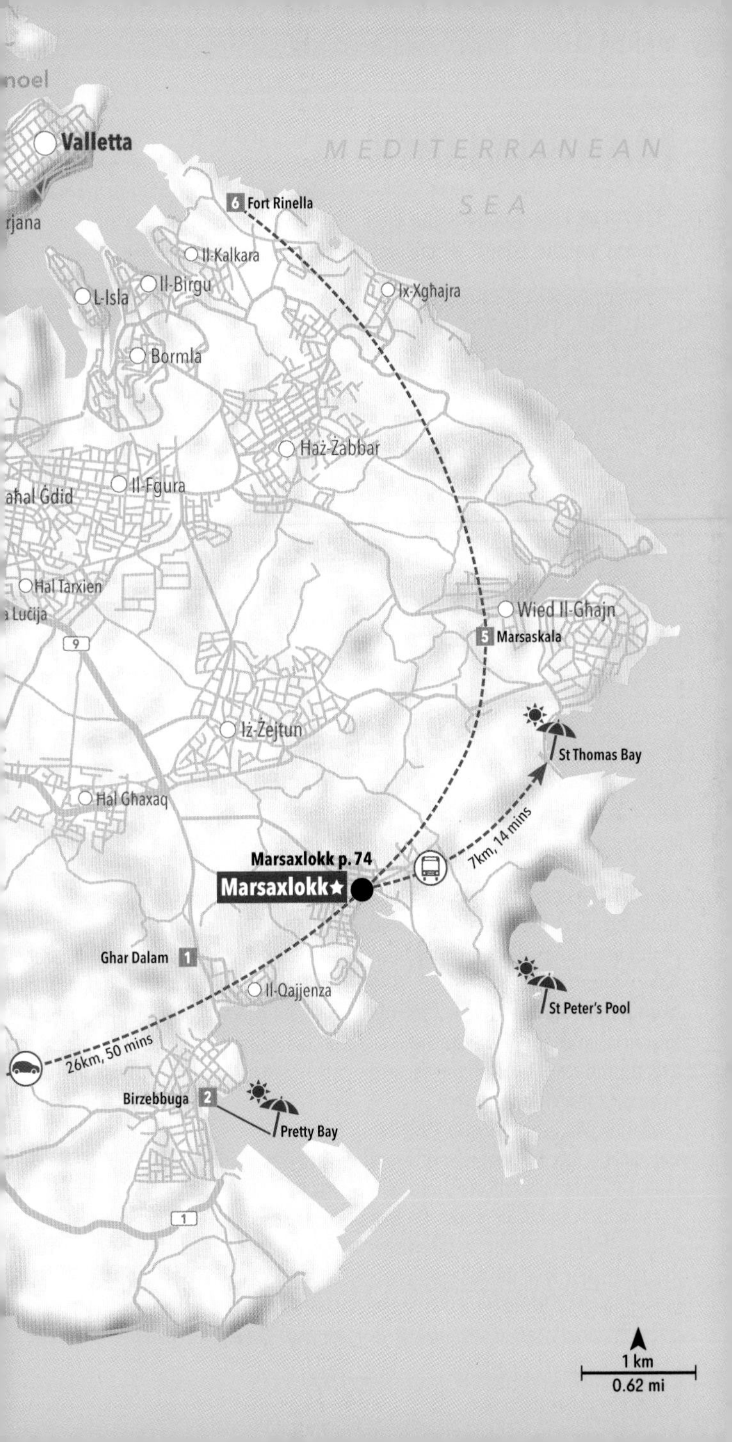

MEDITERRANEAN SEA

Valletta

6 Fort Rinella

Il-Kalkara

L-Isla

Il-Birgu

Ix-Xghajra

Bormla

Haż-Żabbar

Il-Fgura

ħal Ġdid

Hal Tarxien

a Luċija

9

Wied Il-Għajn

5 Marsaskala

Iż-Żejtun

St Thomas Bay

Hal Għaxaq

Marsaxlokk p. 74
Marsaxlokk★

7km, 14 mins

Ghar Dalam **1**

St Peter's Pool

Il-Qajjenza

26km, 50 mins

Birzebbuga **2**

Pretty Bay

1

▲
N
1 km
0.62 mi

MARSAXLOKK

(□ N10) ★ **Marsaxlokk is the only location on the island where you**

hungry guests. No wonder then that most of the photos of Malta that appear in glossy magazines are taken in Marsaxlokk; there are no second homes to blight the idyllic scene.

Get the pick of the catch at Marsaxlokk's daily market

can still see colourful fishing boats bobbing on the water and moored along the quay where fishing families mend their nets. The promenade is lined with fish restaurants, and the low-rise houses are dominated by the dome and towers of the village church.

Marsaxlokk is the only working fishing village left on the island. More than 130 fishing boats are registered here and, unlike in most coastal resorts, they put to sea in the winter too. The majority of the village's population makes its living from fish: some catch it; others sell it or serve it to

Fish taverns and other good restaurants attract many locals in the evenings and at weekends, but there are no late-night bars and clubs to disturb the peace. A daily market is held on the quay; come on Sunday for the chance to browse the greatest number of stalls.

SIGHTSEEING

FISHING BOATS

Two-thirds of Maltese fishing fleets are based in Marsaxlokk. Most Maltese boats have eyes – not real ones of course. These are painted on both sides of the bow to bring luck, ward off evil and symbolise alertness. To provide additional heavenly protection, nearly all the boats are given religious names, such as Mother Teresa, for example. Most are traditional rowing boats with mast and sail, but the power of muscle and wind has now been replaced by a motor. When they have the time and inclination, some of the fishermen run short tours of the bay in their boats. Keep a look out for them on the quayside to the west.

EATING & DRINKING

IPLACE

The only place on Malta where each guest is given an iPad, and that goes for kids too. Use it to browse the menu, order your meal without calling for a waiter, and get your bill. The iPad remains on the table the whole time, allowing you to surf the net, send emails or play on one of the many games. If you've had enough of the fishing boats, pick a table inside. Some of the tables even have their own screens where you can watch films or upload your own holiday photos. Almost as appealing is the fact that the international cuisine is excellent and reasonably priced – and, if you're struggling with the technology, there are efficient waiters to take your order instead. *Daily | Triq Il-Wilga | tel. 21 65 41 14 | iplace.com.mt | €–€€*

INSIDER TIP
Check out your holiday snaps

TERRONE

Fine dining with friends: the restaurant specialises in large platters for guests to share, serving meat or fish, mussels, scampi or langoustines. Most of the ingredients used are regional and organic. The cress and dill, for example, are grown on the Delimara peninsula. *Daily | Triq Il-Wilga | tel. 27 04 26 56 | terrone. com.mt | €–€€*

THREE SISTERS

A waterfront location on the quayside. Meat and fish are accompanied by your choice of side dishes: salad or vegetables, chips or roast potatoes. Tip: try the freshly filled calamari. *Daily | Triq Il-Wilga (coastal road) | tel. 27 65 65 01 | €*

BEACHES

DELIMARA PENINSULA

An electricity power station blights the view of the bay directly in front of Marsaxlokk. But on the other side of the peninsula are three hidden rocky coves: the much-loved 🌟 St Peter's Pool, plus Long Bay and Slugs Pool. You can get there in 20–30 minutes by following a series of footpaths. Take swim shoes with you.

HARBOUR BEACH

Hardly anyone does it, but it's possible to bathe right next to the fishing port. The shingle beach stretches for 200 m / 650ft along the east side of the harbour, right behind the village houses.

AROUND MARSAXLOKK

1 GHAR DALAM ☂

3km (2 miles) / approx. 10 mins by car, 15 mins by bus from Marsaxlokk

Sounds eerie: Ar Dalam (as it is pronounced) means Cave of Darkness. In fact, it isn't entirely dark inside anymore. The cave is 145m / 475ft long, but the first third is illuminated and easy to access.

When the cave was first examined, it was found to contain numerous bones from extinct animals that lived on Malta up to 10,000 years ago. They included dwarf elephants (the smallest of which was no larger than a Saint Bernard dog), hippos, red deer, wolves, foxes, bears, toads and dormice. It is thought that, during the Ice Age, a land bridge existed between Malta and what is now Italy, and that animals moved south across it as the ice approached.

On higher levels, researchers also found several shards of ancient pottery that suggest the island was first settled around 5,200 BCE.

Many animal bones can still be identified on the floor of the cave. A few items found in Ghar Dalam are on display in the modest *museum area* in the ticket office; intact skeletons from more recent times provide a point of comparison. *Daily 9am–5pm | admission 5 euros | right-hand side of the road from Valletta towards Birzebbuga | ⏱ 30 mins | 🕮 N10*

2 BIRZEBBUGA

7km (4.5 miles) / approx. 15 mins by car, 20 mins by bus from Marsaxlokk

🐦 Pretty Bay in Birzebugga (pop. 7,600) offers a unique bathing experience. Don't be misled by the name – the view is anything but pretty: plunge into the water from the short, yet wide sandy beach and you'll be swimming directly in front of Malta's container port, Kalafrana. If you'd rather give swimming a miss, then simply take a leisurely stroll along the promenade to watch the hive of maritime activity that goes on all day long. The port handles 1.5 million containers every year, with 2,200 container vessels docking here each year – that's the equivalent of six a day. **Use the "Marine Traffic" app to find out where the** enormous container ships have come from and where they are going next. 🕮 *N10–11*

> INSIDER TIP
> **Ship ahoy!**

3 HAGAR QIM & MNAJDRA ⭐

15km (9 miles) / approx. 25 mins by car, at least 1 hr by bus from Marsaxlokk

An absolute must-see, even for tourists who claim not to be interested in culture. These two temple complexes date back 3,500 years and are nestled in a dreamy setting far away from the nearest village.

Pronounced Agar Imm and M-Nidra, the temples are surrounded by fields and meadows, with the nearby sea adding to the colourful scene. Futuristic-style canopies have recently been erected over the temples to protect them from the elements – they make a great backdrop for a selfie.

These sites provide the ideal opportunity for visitors not merely to gaze at these ancient temple complexes, but also to understand them.

Hagar Qim possesses almost all the characteristics that are typical of 24in thick and weighs more than 20 tons.

The size, symmetry and beauty of the main temple of Hagar Qim are impressive. Beyond the entrance, the first of the kidney-shaped rooms of the temple has carefully shaped window stones giving access to two side

A voluptuous Stone Age sculpture on display in the visitor centre at Hagar Qim

Neolithic Maltese temples. The technical achievement of the temple builders from 5,000 years ago, who had neither metal tools nor pulleys, is astounding. But equally stunning is their refined aesthetic sensibility. On first inspection of the temple, a solitary block of stone, unusually tall at 5.2m / 17ft, catches the eye. Was it a phallic symbol for a fertility cult? Next to it lies the largest of all the stones used for a temple on Malta; it is over 4m / 13ft high, 7m / 23ft long, 60cm / chambers. Several altar stones, decorated all over with perforations, are also discernible. This chamber also holds a copy of the famous Altar of Hagar Qim; the original altar is on display in the National Museum in Valletta. All four sides of the altar feature a relief of a plant growing out of a pot. A little further on, you will see two altars that are shaped like mushrooms. The number of altars may be an indication of the great importance of sacrifices to the culture of the

Neolithic temples. A striking feature of the site is the number of trilithon structures, consisting of two vertical stones with a horizontal lintel laid on top of them.

Oracles were probably consulted in the temples. At least this is how researchers interpret the oval structure made from low slabs of stone in the northeast corner of the temple complex. In one of these slabs they found a hole, 40cm / 16in above the floor, which connected to a tiny chamber behind. It is probable that a consecrated priestess sat in the smaller chamber and spoke to the people assembled in the oval space.

A distance of only 500m / 1,640ft towards the coast separates Hagar Qim from the temple site of Mnajdra.

Of all the temple complexes on Malta, this one is closest to the sea, and it also has a surprisingly clear layout. Perhaps of most interest is the fact that the form of the temple roof is clearly discernible from inside the main kidney-shaped chamber. The masonry of large, horizontal stones has survived here to a height of 4.3m / 14ft, creating a layered structure like an upturned beehive. Yet there was no dome at the top because the uppermost part was probably finished off with wooden beams and clay. *April–Sept daily 8am–6pm, Oct–March daily 9am–5pm | combined ticket 10 euros | ⏱ 1–1.5 hrs*

Opposite Hagar Qim Temple and above the visitor centre is a little garden that is lovingly tended by its

Don't miss the natural spectacle of the Blue Grotto

owner Jane. In its midst lies *Restaurant Hagar Qim (daily | tel. 21 42 41 16 | €€)*. The restaurant

sometimes hosts a karaoke show on Friday evenings, and on Saturday nights there is often live country and western music. Call ahead to check. The lunch buffet on Sundays is very popular with Maltese locals. ▢ *K10–11*

4 BLUE GROTTO ★

12km (7.5 miles) / approx. 20 mins by car, 1 hr by bus from Marsaxlokk

No holiday to the Mediterranean would be complete without a blue grotto. Malta's keeps many local families in business. They run cafés and snack bars in *Wied iz-Zurrieq*, the boarding point for open-top boat excursions to the grotto. In calm weather, one boat leaves every ten minutes. They ferry passengers along the steep coastline and into several sea caves, where the reflected sunlight and an abundance of orange algae creates a varied play of colour. The Blue Grotto is the largest cave, at 30m / 100ft high and 90m / 300ft in circumference. The effects of light are especially strong here in the mornings. Trips may be cancelled in bad weather, so call ahead to check. *Tel. 21 68 04 04 | duration of boat trip 20–25 mins | tickets 9 euros | ▢ L11*

5 MARSASKALA

8km (5 miles) / at least 10 mins by car, 30 mins by bus from Marsaxlokk

A coastal village that resembles a balloon: full to bursting with life in August and at weekends, but deflated at other times. Why? Because many Maltese own a weekend home here, and there are virtually no hotels for tourists. The only attraction is ☀ *St Thomas Bay* to the southwest of Marsaskala. Locals come here to enjoy the 70-m / 230-ft stretch of sandy beach and the flat rocks and concrete slabs that reach out into the sea. ▢ *O9*

6 FORT RINELLA

10km (6.5 miles) / approx. 20 mins by car, 40 mins by bus from Marsaxlokk

Are you free at 2pm in the afternoon? Do you appreciate British eccentricity? Then head to this 19th-century fort *(Mon–Sat 10am–5pm | guided tour 12 euros | fortrinella.com)*, where a sergeant dressed in traditional uniform will explain about the poor living conditions experienced by the British soldiers who were once stationed here with their families. Cannons are fired and the cavalry are called to arms. There's even the chance for visitors to fire a musket (for a donation of 5 euros).

With a bit of luck, there might be an even bigger show taking place over the fence a few hundred metres to the south, if a scene for a blockbuster film or an advert is being shot on the huge outdoor water feature at the *Mediterranean Film Studios*. From the studios, you can also see the high-rise buildings of *Smart City*, Malta's IT park.

If you want to visit Smart City, it's best to wait for a special event or go on a Sunday, when lots of people gather to enjoy the pond and the fountains. ▢ *N8*

CENTRAL MALTA

Away from its coastal resorts, Malta is still a beauty. Perched high on a rocky outcrop overlooking vineyards, Mdina has only three hotels, the largest of which has just 17 rooms. Inside this tiny walled city, horse-drawn carriages replace cars, there are old palaces instead of supermarkets, and cafés on the city ramparts offer fabulous views. The adjoining city of Rabat exists on two levels: one above and one below ground; one for today, the other for eternity.

Decorative architecture in Mdina

All around, the countryside is a patchwork of fields and meadows, with sea views by day and clear starry skies at night. There are stone walls everywhere and a quarry for good measure, not to mention 200-m / 656-ft high cliffs that plunge into the sea below. You could easily spend the day walking or sunbathing in these beautiful surroundings – perhaps you won't want to do anything else. However, there are also two open-air clubs that are filled with young Maltese in the summer months.

CENTRAL MALTA

MARCO POLO HIGHLIGHTS

★ **MDINA**
Malta's "quiet city" – no traffic allowed
➤ p. 84

★ **CATACOMBS**
Discover the secrets of Malta's underworld in the enigmatic catacombs
➤ p. 87

★ **FONTANELLA TEA GARDEN**
A gourmet paradise for lovers of cake, located on the city walls ➤ p. 89

★ **DINGLI CLIFFS**
Natural beauty and fresh sea air on stunning coastal cliffs ➤ p. 90

★ **BUSKETT GARDENS**
Malta's most beautiful woodland, with pines and palm trees ➤ p. 92

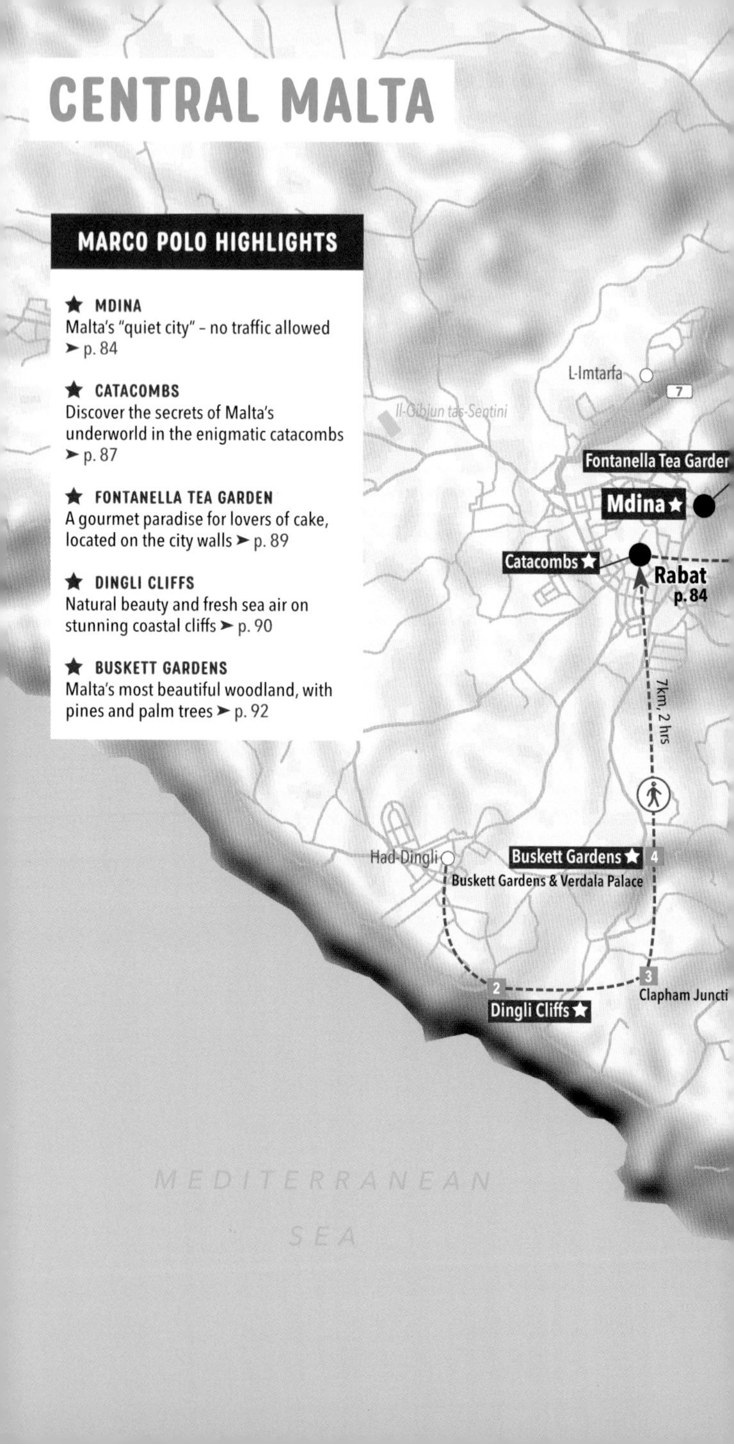

L-Imtarfa

7

Il-Ġibjun ta-Seqtini

Fontanella Tea Garder

Mdina ★

Catacombs ★

Rabat
p. 84

1

7km, 2 hrs

Had-Dingli

Buskett Gardens ★ 4
Buskett Gardens & Verdala Palace

2
Dingli Cliffs ★

3
Clapham Juncti

M E D I T E R R A N E A N

S E A

1 Aviation Museum

7 Mosta

In-Naxxar

L-Iklin

Hal Lija

Birkirkara

Hal Balzan

8 Attard

6km, 60 mins

21

MALTA

Haż-Żebbug

4km, 10 mins

5 Siggiewi

L-Imqabba

Gibjun San Niklaw

Il-Qrendi

6 Ghar Lapsi

2 km
1.24 mi

MDINA & RABAT

(□ J8-9) **A different kind of city: first take a stroll through almost car-free ★ Mdina (pop. 370), which was the main residence of the Maltese nobility when the Order of St John ruled the island. Notice**

and the locals reclaim Rabat briefly before going early to bed.

Together, the two towns occupy the flat-topped foothills of the Dingli Plateau, which were settled in antiquity. The walls of the Roman town of *Melite* encircled what is now Mdina and half of Rabat, but by the time the Arabs conquered Malta in 870, these walls were in ruins. The city's fortifications were rebuilt by the

Narrow streets and pretty facades – Mdina's old town is picture-perfect

the beautiful architectural details: huge brass doorknockers, exuberant entrances, wooden bay windows. Then visit the working and farming town of Rabat (pop. 11,500), where everyday life carries on regardless of the daytrippers. At night, stillness returns to Mdina

Muslims and, again, in the 12th century by the Normans. During the Great Siege of 1565, the invading Turkish forces barely threatened the town, which meant its inhabitants were able to send supplies to the Knights of St John and pass their messages on to Sicily.

When Valletta was built, Mdina declined in importance, as people moved to the new capital of the island. Only the Maltese nobility kept their palaces here and deliberately shunned the city of the Knights of St John. Today, rather than individual buildings, it is the overall ensemble of historic palaces and bastions, alleys, corners and squares in Mdina which leaves the most lasting impression.

SIGHTSEEING IN MDINA

TOUR OF THE TOWN

Start your tour of the town by visiting the obligatory tourist attractions, but then head off the beaten track to stroll around the less significant and less well-known parts of this fortified town.

First, hop in one of the horse-drawn carriages *(official price 35 euros for 20 mins, price is open to negotiation)* that wait for tourists at the point where Rabat and Mdina meet. It's the perfect way to spend a late afternoon or evening. Then, proceed over the bridge guarded by two stone lions. Take the opportunity for a selfie in front of the Baroque main gate from 1724; if you time it right, you may catch a carriage passing through in the background. You can pick up a free town map from *Tourist Information (daily from 9am, Mon–Fri until 6.30pm, Sat until 5.30pm, Sun until 1pm),* which is housed in the Torre dello Stendardo behind the main gate. This signal tower was built in 1750; a fiery beacon would be lit at the top to send a signal to Valletta that enemies were approaching. Lots of multimedia shows are advertised in the tourist information office, but none of them really justifies the high ticket prices.

Mdina's main street starts a few steps beyond the Torre dell Stendardo. *Villegaignon Street* is 230m / 755ft long and lined with churches and palaces. Of particular note on the left-hand side, between Inguanez and Mesquita streets, is *Casa Inguanez*, seat of the oldest noble family on Malta. To this day, the kings of Spain have the unrestricted right to reside here, although they have not exercised this privilege since 1927. From the city's main square, *Misrah San Pawl*, there is an unobstructed view of the cathedral (which you will visit later on this tour).

For now, continue past the Carmelite monastery and several old palaces to *Misrah is-Sur*, from where you can access the town's fortifications and take in the stunning views over the island. This is a good spot for a break, with three restaurants located right on the city walls.

From *Palazzo de Piro*, you can head back down to take a look inside *St Paul's Cathedral*, built in 1700 *(Mon–Fri 9.30am–4.30pm, Sat 9.30am–3.30pm | admission 5 euros incl. cathedral museum).* The floor is covered with colourful marble inlay work indicating the tombs of nobles and clerics who are buried here. Scenes from the lives of the apostles St Peter and St Paul decorate the vaulted ceiling, and the main altar is an opulent piece made from marble and lapis lazuli.

Now return to the main street, Triq

Villegaignon, and head down narrow Triq San Pietru, leaving the souvenir shops behind you. Away from the major sights, this is where the locals live within the centuries-old walls.

Take a break in *Il-Mina tal-Griegi*, a tiny square where you can rest under the shade of Malta's craziest fig tree with a refreshing drink from the kiosk opposite. Leave Mdina by the *Greek's Gate*, the city's second gateway, to reach Rabat and the Domus Romana.

INSIDER TIP
Take a break

MUSEUM OF NATURAL HISTORY

This museum is a popular outing for Maltese school pupils, who come to study the human skeleton and other animals. The island's inhabitants were once avid bird-hunters, so the museum also exhibits hundreds of stuffed birds. *Daily 9am–5pm | admission 5 euros | St Publius Square | 15–20 mins*

PALAZZO FALSON

In this two-story palazzo, the core of which dates back to the 13th century, over 3,500 artworks, weapons and antiques are on show. The collection was amassed by Captain Olof Frederick Gollcher, the palace's last owner. *Tue–Sun 10am–5pm | admission 10 euros incl. audio guide | Villegaignon Street | palazzofalson.com | 20–30 mins*

PALAZZO DE PIRO

This 17th-century palazzo, which has been modified several times over the years, was recently completely renovated in order to host temporary exhibitions and concerts. It also houses the café-bar *Xpresso (daily |*

€€), which offers an impressive view over large portions of the island from its location on the city walls. *Daily | 3 Triq is-Sur | tel. 20 10 05 60*

SIGHTSEEING IN RABAT

DOMUS ROMANA

The last inhabitants of this Roman townhouse died almost 2,000 years ago. Excavated in 1881, the remaining ruins give a good impression of how affluent Romans once lived. The layout illustrates the vast size of the complex, but the house's showpiece is the splendid mosaic flooring, which has a depiction of two doves drinking from a golden bowl at its centre.

The ingenuity of the mosaic artists in creating optical illusions can be seen in one of the display cases: three mosaic rhombuses combine to form a two-dimensional hexagon which resembles a three-dimensional cube to the human eye. *Daily 9am–5pm | admission 6 euros | Museum Esplanade | ⊘ 20–30 mins*

CASA BERNARD

Inquisitive tourists are warmly welcomed inside this aristocratic residence from the 16th century. Without them, the owners, Georges and Josette Magri, would not be able to afford the upkeep on their home. They often personally guide visitors around the rooms, enthusiastically explaining the stories behind the furniture, artworks and paintings. *Mon–Sat 10am–4pm | admission 8 euros | 46 St Paul Street | Rabat | casabernard.eu | ⊘ 40–50 mins*

CATACOMBS ★

Dive down into the underworld. Beneath large parts of Rabat lies another town, a realm of the dead: the catacombs. Pagans, Christians and Jews dug out the rock in the fourth and fifth centuries and buried their dead there in various rocky tombs. Early Christians also came here regularly to host *agapes* (commemorative meals) on special stone tables to honour the dead. The atmosphere and smells of decomposition must have been extremely disturbing.

Today, the catacombs belong to several private landowners and are not all open to the public. It's worth visiting three of them: *St Paul's Catacombs (daily 9am–5pm | admission 4 euros | St Agatha Street | ⊘ 30–40 mins)* are the largest on Malta, with around 900

Medallion of the Virgin Mary on Palazzo de Piro

surviving graves and 900m / 0.5 miles of passageways. At the heart of these catacombs is a hall with an *agape table* hewn out of the rock at each end. The chamber is flanked on three sides by passages and rooms containing various types of graves. The most common are the simple *loculi graves*. These were usually a rectangular or curved niche in the wall that could be covered with a stone, though sometimes they were simply a covered shaft in the floor. Most of them were probably used as children's graves. More elaborate tombs were the preserve of the well-off. For *canopy graves,* a section of rock was hollowed out so that its covering looked like a vaulted canopy. Usually there was space for two bodies beneath it, maybe a married couple.

St Agatha's Catacombs (guided visits Mon–Fri 9am–noon and 1–4.30pm, Sat 9am–12.30pm | admission 5 euros | St Agatha Street | stagathamalta.com | ⏱ 30 mins) are far narrower than the St Paul Catacombs and are not recommended for claustrophobics. However, their late Roman and medieval frescoes make these catacombs a must-visit for art lovers. The Roman frescoes from the third to fifth centuries depict pelicans as a symbol of Christ and peacocks as an embodiment of eternal life. There are also images of the Virgin Mary and St Paul and 13 representations of St Agatha. Most visitors are puzzled by images of St Agatha holding a bowl containing two breasts. What do they mean? They are, in fact, her own breasts,

INSIDER TIP
A macabre message

which were cut from her body by her torturers during her martyrdom.

During World War II, the catacombs were converted into air-raid shelters and used as a refuge from the bombs. The best example of this is in the *Wignacourt Catacombs (daily 9.30am–5pm | admission 5 euros | access from the Wignacourt Museum on Paris Square | wignacourtmuseum.com | ⏱ 30–40 mins).* These are connected to St Paul's Grotto, where the apostle is supposed to have stayed during his visit to Malta in CE 50. Every pope who comes to Malta visits the grotto, most recently Pope Benedict in 2010.

EATING & DRINKING

BACCHUS

These 17th-century vaults are just the place to soak up some romantic chivalric atmosphere. The Maltese knights may have stored ammunition here, but today you can savour fine Mediterranean cuisine with influences from around the world. *Daily | 1 Inguanez Street | Mdina | tel. 21 45 49 81 | bacchus.com.mt | €€€*

COOGI'S

Just a few steps from the well-trodden tourist path, Coogi's is a hidden gem. Five tables on the city wall, two small courtyards and a medieval vaulted cellar – the entire restaurant has been lovingly designed as an intimate escape from the hustle and bustle. It caters for vegetarians and

INSIDER TIP
Escape the hustle and bustle

Time travel: head down into the underworld to visit Rabat's catacombs

vegans, as well as serving gluten-free beer. The flavours of Piemont and Malta are very much in evidence. Try the carrot and leek flan in anchovy-garlic sauce (*sformatino*) or the fried rabbit liver. *Daily, until 3pm only in winter | 5 St Agatha's Esplanade | Mdina | tel. 21 45 99 87 | €€*

DON MESQUITA

If you're just feeling a bit peckish, then this tiny wine bar in Mdina is the right place to go. You'll feel as though you're in a Maltese living room as you sample a glass of Maltese wine accompanied by sausage and salami specialities, sun-dried tomatoes, olives, *bigilla*, goat's cheese and bread. You'll eat just enough to satisfy your appetite without making a big dent in your budget. *Mon–Sat 10am–3pm only | Pjazza Mesquita 5A | tel. 27 02 66 40 | €*

FONTANELLA TEA GARDEN ★

Less intimate, but with an enviable location right on the city bastion, this restaurant affords views across half the island. Every one of the 250 seats in the tea garden is nearly always fully booked thanks to sweet-toothed visitors, who come to enjoy the wide selection of cakes and desserts – there are over 25 varieties to choose from. Rather than ask the waiter for the bill, you pay at the counter in the courtyard. *Daily | 1 Bastion Street | Mdina | tel. 21 45 42 64 | €*

TA' DONI DELI

On the street are four tables for two surrounded by rosemary-filled flower pots, with more rosemary decorating the tables. Inside, the small counter is like a mini delicatessen, boasting an array of locally sourced ingredients and fillings for sandwiches and platters, plus organic teas, homemade wines and a craft beer brewed on Gozo. A jazz soundtrack completes the scene. *Mon–Sat 10am–6pm | Triq San Pawl/ Triq Doni | Rabat | tel. 27 61 52 70*

There is absolutely nothing going on in Mdina and Rabat in the evenings – but, in summer, young locals flock to two enormous clubs just outside town, with capacity for up to 10,000 partygoers. *Uno Malta (unomalta.com)* and *Gianpula (gianpula.com)* have ten different dancing areas between them, and live acts perform almost every weekend. Particularly sought after is the Roof Top Lounge at Gianpula, thanks to its swimming pools with their white day beds. You'll only get in with a reservation.

INSIDER TIP
The party starts here

THE RISING SUN

A lifesaver for those who don't want to go to bed early despite the lack of nightclubs. There's classic rock and blues on the playlist until 4am; the bar is well-stocked, and the clientele are good-humoured and talkative. *Triq San Pawl 71 | Rabat*

AROUND MDINA & RABAT

🔲 AVIATION MUSEUM

3km (2 miles) / approx. 30 mins on foot from Mdina

Take a seat in the cockpit of a BAC 1–11, an aeroplane now retired from charter flight service. Get a close-up look at a DC-3, the plane that was used during the Berlin airlift, or at a Spitfire that was part of the Allied invasion of Sicily. The museum exhibits 23 historic planes in total. *Daily 9am–5pm, Sun until 1pm only in summer | admission 7 euros | Hut 161 | Ta' Qali | maltaaviationmuseum.com | ⏱ 30–40 mins*

🔲 DINGLI CLIFFS ★

8km (5 miles) / approx. 15 mins by car, 30 min by bus from Mdina

Do you yearn for a dramatic landscape? The Dingli Cliffs will satisfy your longing. The 200-m / 656-ft cliffs drop directly into the sea for several kilometres along the coast. In places, the sheer horizontal rock face is interrupted by terraces of cultivated land close to the water's edge, which were one used for intensive agriculture.

It is forbidden to descend the cliffs, because the land below is in private ownership and is frequented by Malta's illegal bird hunters. But the steep cliffs remain a visual highlight all the same. A narrow road leads

The road that runs along the top of the Dingli Cliffs is known as Triq Panoramika

along the clifftops, which are dotted with just several benches, a tiny chapel and several radars belonging to Maltese air traffic control. Even the inland village of Dingli is a discreet distance from this natural beauty. Those who want to explore on foot can come by bus and walk along the coastal trail, past Clapham Junction and the Buskett Gardens, to Rabat.

A good place for an extended break en route is *The Cliffs (Wed–Mon | Vizitaturi | near the main air traffic control radar | tel. 21 45 54 70 | thecliffs. com.mt | €€)*, a restaurant that serves rabbit roulade and a "One Kilometer Platter". Everything on the platter comes from within a kilometre radius of the restaurant. The building itself is

SIDER TIP
Zero food miles

highly energy efficient, and there are plans to offer bikes for hire in the near future.

The restaurant also offers free *Dingli Cliff Tours (Winter Wed & Fri 11am, summer Thu 6.30pm | donations requested | pre-booking necessary: tel. 79 64 23 80 | thecliffs.com.mt)*. After a short audio-visual presentation, local volunteers take visitors (maximum 25) on a two-hour tour of the area. *H–J9*

▣ CLAPHAM JUNCTION
4km (2.5 miles) / approx. 10 mins by car, 30 mins by bus from Mdina
Puzzle fans are drawn to the deep tracks that have been scoured into the rocky surface near Buskett Gardens; parallel ruts in the stone up to 40cm / 16in deep cross and branch off each

other like a system of railway tracks. Under British rule, the bizarre site was given the nickname "Clapham Junction" after the railway hub in south London. It is believed that Bronze Age people hewed the tracks out of the limestone rock – but the question remains as to why? Were they really used as sliders for carts? Where did they come from and where did they lead to? Nobody knows for sure, so your guess is as good as any.

A signpost at a crossing near the *Buskett Forest Aparthotel* shows the way. Follow the drive for about 200m / 656ft past a right-hand bend as far as little cube-shaped house. Here, turn right onto a path across the fields and, after a few paces, you'll reach Clapham Junction on a slope on the left-hand side. *Free access* | ⏱ *20–30 mins* | 📖 *J10*

4 BUSKETT GARDENS & VERDALA PALACE

4km (2.5 miles) / approx. 10 mins by car, 30 mins by bus from Mdina

This is the only place on Malta that can justifiably claim to be a woodland. Also known as the Boschetto, ★ *Buskett Gardens* is a lovely wooded area that was laid out in about 1570 as a hunting ground for Grand Master Lascaris. Plentiful water irrigates vines, palms, pines and Aleppo pines, and mulberry, lemon and orange trees. In summer, many Maltese come here for a short walk and an extended picnic, and on the weekend before 29 June a big popular festival takes place here.

Inland, the *Verdala Palace* lords it over the gardens from its majestic

position on one of the highest points of the island. In 1586, Grand Master Hugues Loubenx de Verdale commissioned Gerolamo Cassar, an architect who was much employed by the Order, to build a small palace using stone taken from a moat that was dug around the site. The resulting building resembles a castle with four corner towers. After the Knights of St John left the island, the palace was used as a military prison and a silk factory, among other functions. Since 1987, it has been used as the summer

Mosta's Rotunda, including its gigantic dome, was constructed by the town's inhabitants

residence of the President of Malta. *Palace closed to visitors | free access to the park |* 🕮 *J9*

5 SIGGIEWI

5km (3 miles) / approx. 10 mins by car, 20 mins by bus from Mdina
Siggiewi (pop. 7,400) is the location of a genuinely interesting visitor attraction in a quarry, *The Limestone Heritage Park (Mon–Fri 9am–4pm, Sat 9am–noon | admission 7 euros | Triq Mons M. Azzopardi | limestoneheritage. com).* Watch a short slide show and then follow an audio-guided tour through a small disused quarry to find out all about Maltese limestone. Wax figures, old equipment and vehicles bring the site to life. There's also a cafe-teria and souvenir shop; in the summer, there are folklore shows with a Maltese buffet in the evening. 🕮 *K9–10*

6 GHAR LAPSI

10km (6 miles) / approx. 15 mins by car, 30 mins by bus from Mdina
Another curious bathing spot. Harbouring a few fishing boats in

summer, this tiny cove (pronounced "Ar Lapsi") has rocky promontories for sunbathing and a handful of shady patches of sand to accommodate a maximum of 20 people – and these fill up quickly. You can watch – or even join – the divers and snorkelers who gather here to explore the island's underwater world.

The cove has a simple cafeteria (€) and a super restaurant: *Blue Creek (daily, closed 4–6pm | tel. 21 46 28 00 | bluecreekmalta. com | €€)* Sitting on the terrace, you'll feel as though you're on the prow of a ship heading out to the high seas. It's particularly special at sunset and under starry skies. It goes without saying that freshly caught fish is served at these fine-dining tables. ⌑ *K11*

> **INSIDER TIP**
> **Cruise ship atmosphere on land**

7 MOSTA (⌑ K8)

5km (3 miles) / approx. 10 mins by car, 30 mins by bus from Mdina
Malta is full of wonders. The town of Mosta (pop. 17,400) witnessed a miracle in 1942 when a German aircraft bomb hit the massive dome (54m / 177ft in diameter, 60m / 196ft in height) of the Rotunda but failed to explode, saving the lives of the people in the church at the time. Today, the bomb is seen as proof of the hand of God and is on display as a memorial in the vestry of the church *(daily 9am–noon and 3–5pm | free admission | ⌚ 15–20 mins)*. The enormous church was financed by the inhabitants of Mosta themselves,

and built by hand between 1833 and 1860.

About 150m / 492ft further along the road towards St Paul's Bay is the restaurant ⚑ *Ta' Marija (Tue–Sun, Mon dinner only | Constitution Street | tel. 21 43 44 44 | tamarija.com | €€),* which has the largest selection of Maltese specialities on the whole island, including excellent Maltese coffee. For authentic folklore shows, there's no better venue than this. Be sure to book your table and your hotel transfer in advance *(55 euros, incl. fixed menu, water, wine and transfer).* ⌑ *K8*

> **INSIDER TIP**
> **A kitsch treat**

8 ATTARD

3km (2 miles) / approx. 30 mins on foot from Mdina
The inland town of Attard (pop. 9,500) is the location of the President's palace. As a sign of the President's attachment to his people, locals are invited to walk freely around the grounds, stroll through the courtyard and taste herbs and vegetables from the presidential garden in the cafeteria, proudly known as *The President's Kitchen (daily 9am–7pm, July–Sept 9am–2pm, 6–10pm | €).* Maltese family life is on display for all to see in the large playground adjoining the cafeteria and in the shady park with its turtle pond, gigantic yuccas, floss-silk trees and numerous cats. And if you like, you can admire the exterior of the opulent presidential residence, *San Anton Palace*, which was built in 1636 for Grand Master Antoine de Paule. ⌑ *K8*

SHOPPING

TA' QALI

In many places, these old aircraft hangars and World War II Nissan huts, industrial buildings and wasteland would have been flattened to make room for new residential buildings. But the Maltese are practical folk, and decided to convert this former RAF airfield into a craft village. The talented producers sell a diverse range of unique yet affordable items. Tourists like coming here to find a special "made in Malta" souvenir to take back home. Don't miss the glass-blowers working their magic at *Mdina Glass* and *Valletta Glassblowers*. Entrance is free.

The craft village lies next to *Ta' Qali National Park*, Malta's newest protected green space, which is unfortunately blighted by too much concrete. The park is the site of the *National Stadium,* where Malta's national football team suffers many home defeats. The stadium also hosts Maltese Premier League games, often showing several matches back-to-back on the same day. For the match dates, visit *maltafootball.com*.

WELLNESS

ATHENAEUM SPA

Most of the spa users are locals with an annual membership. Some value the proximity to the Presidential Palace; others enjoy the beautiful garden, but everyone appreciates the range of treatments on offer. A favourite among couples is the one-hour "Hugs & Kisses" programme, which even the pope himself couldn't complain about. *Mon–Fri 6am–10pm, Sat/Sun 8am–7pm | day membership 25 euros, Hugs & Kisses 120 euros per couple | Hotel Corinthia Palace | De Paule Avenue | San Anton | tel. 25 44 30 01 | corinthia.com*

INSIDER TIP
Wellness for two

You'll find delicate silverwork and other handicrafts at T' Qali

NORTHWEST MALTA

WHERE TO FIND MALTA'S BEACHES

Only in the north does Malta reveal itself to be an island with beautiful sandy beaches that are perfect for bathing. But you won't find uniform rows of sunbeds even here, since each beach has its own quite distinct character.

What's more, the beaches are not backed by towns and resorts – with the exception of Mellieha Bay, accommodation is located elsewhere, most of it in the resort of Bugibba–Qawra. This has hardly any beach to speak of but countless bars, pubs and restaurants.

Comino's Blue Lagoon

Tourist infrastructure is concentrated in this area, leaving plenty of room for nature in the rest of the region. You'll see farmers cultivating the small fields, and herds of sheep and goats grazing the scrub. It's an ideal landscape for hiking, biking and even riding.

Reminders of the region's history are most in evidence in the large village of Mellieha and along the coast in the form of lookout towers. One of the towers stands on the tiny islet of Comino, between Malta and Gozo, where the Blue Lagoon is always worth a trip in summer.

NORTHWEST MALTA

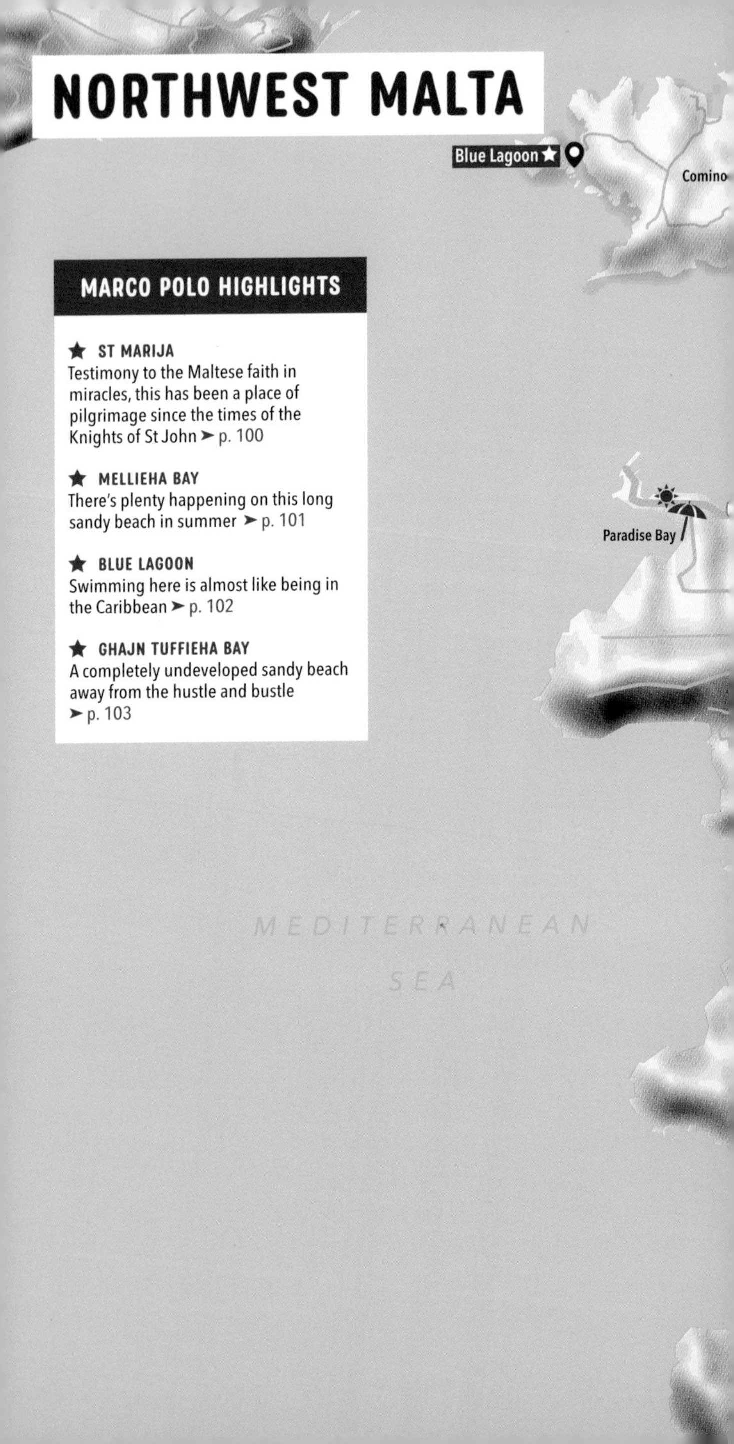

Blue Lagoon ★ ◉

Comino

MARCO POLO HIGHLIGHTS

★ **ST MARIJA**
Testimony to the Maltese faith in miracles, this has been a place of pilgrimage since the times of the Knights of St John ➤ p. 100

★ **MELLIEHA BAY**
There's plenty happening on this long sandy beach in summer ➤ p. 101

★ **BLUE LAGOON**
Swimming here is almost like being in the Caribbean ➤ p. 102

★ **GHAJN TUFFIEHA BAY**
A completely undeveloped sandy beach away from the hustle and bustle ➤ p. 103

Paradise Bay

MEDITERRANEAN

SEA

Kemmuna

Armier Bay

Mellieha Bay ★

St Marija ★

● **Mellieha**
p. 100

16km, 50-60 mins

Ix-Xemxija

St Paul's Bay
p. 102 ●

Buġibba

38km, 38-44 mins

Il-Manikata

1

GOLDEN BAY

Golden Bay

Ghajn Tuffieha Bay ★

1.5km, 30 mins

2 Mgarr

M A L T A

1 km
0.62 mi

Mellieha: spend the day on the beach, but head to the cliffs for sunset

MELLIEHA

📖 H6 **Mellieha will appeal to visitors who appreciate the quieter life. Spread across a mountain ridge, this small, modern town (pop. 6,500) has just a handful of hotels and restaurants.**

A 10-minute downhill walk leads you to the long sandy beach at Mellieha Bay. Buses can take you to other beaches and to the bars and clubs around St Paul's Bay – something you may want to consider since restaurants close early in Mellieha. You will only need an hour to explore the sights in Mellieha: the church and the air-raid shelters are the only points of interest.

SIGHTSEEING

ST MARIJA ★

The residents of Mellieha don't blame God for the suffering they endured during World War II bombing raids; instead, they come to the underground chapel beneath the parish church to thank Our Lady for the many private miracles she has performed for them. Photos and newspaper cuttings, paintings and votive offerings are on display in the sanctuary, evidence of rescues at sea and of people who survived catastrophic road accidents. The chapel supposedly dates back to CE 409, and the rock painting on the wall is a depiction of Mary allegedly by St Luke the Evangelist. *May–Oct daily 8am–noon and 5–7pm, Nov–April daily 8am–noon and 4–6pm | admission free |* ⏱ *15–20 mins*

MELLIEHA SHELTERS

It's horrible to imagine that 5,000 people were trapped in narrow underground corridors and cells for days at a time as they sought shelter from the bombs during World War II. The tunnels are around 500m / 1,640ft in length, and each person was allocated only 0.6m² / 6.45sq ft of space in these dark, cramped surroundings. *Mon–Sat 9am–3pm | admission 2.40 euros | signposted on the church square | choirandorchestra.org/ heritage-and-culture/wwii-shelters | ⏱15–20 mins*

EATING & DRINKING

BOUQUET GARNI

The menu features freshly made bread, classics like grilled octopus and more creative dishes such as mussels in a coconut-ginger sauce. The chef's family helps out with service in this modern restaurant, which seats a maximum of 30 guests. *Triq Borg Olivier 4 | tel. 21 52 22 34 | €€*

BEACHES

ARMIER BAY ✶⁂

Maltese beachlife – simple and unfussy. Most of the holiday homes around the bay belong to locals and were either built with no planning permission or gained it retrospectively. Cheap and cheerful sun loungers and parasols are available for hire. The two no-frills beach bars attract a young, friendly local crowd. *6km / 3.5 miles from Mellieha | ◫ H4*

MELLIEHA BAY ★ ⁂

Malta's longest sandy beach. Several large yet unobtrusive hotels line the four-lane coastal road, and there is a giant hotel complex on the bay's north shore. Wind- and kitesurfers populate the water, and several beach bars are dotted along the beach. If it gets too busy on the beach, cross to the other side of the road to watch the migrating and over-wintering birds in the *Ghadira Natural Reserve (Nov–May Sat/Sun 10.30am-4.30pm). 2km / 1 mile from Mellieha | ◫ H5*

PARADISE BAY ⁂

A 100-m / 328-ft sandy beach is well hidden below the cliffs a mere 400m / 0.25 miles from the ferry pier in Cirkewwa but invisible from the coastal road. *8km / 5 miles from Mellieha | ◫ G5*

RAMLA BAY

This is the trendy choice. Much of this beach is dominated by a hotel, but the highlight for the public is the *Hola Beach Club (daily 10am–11:30pm | holabeachmalta.com)*, a meeting point for the island's young, rich and beautiful. Get there early to bag one of the white sunbeds which lie under palm trees directly at the water's edge. You can go back to sleep as soon as you arrive. *8km / 5 miles from Mellieha | ◫ G5*

INSIDER TIP
The best seat on the beach

AROUND MELLIEHA

1 COMINO

Approx .15 mins by car or bus to Cirkewwa, then 30 mins by ferry

All good things come in threes. The tiny island of Comino lies in the narrow stretch of sea between Malta and

Gozo and serves as a sought-after bathing spot. In summer, boats regularly ferry passengers here from Cirkewwa, Ramla Bay and Mgarr en route to Gozo. The islet also attracts numerous excursion boats departing from St Paul's Bay and Sliema. They only have one destination in mind: the stunningly beautiful ★ *Blue Lagoon*. Although the sandy beach here is very small and often overcrowded, the beautiful water shimmering in all shades of blue, green and turquoise above golden-yellow sand more than makes up for it. There is no town. The only historic sight on Comino is the *St Marija watchtower* of 1618. ⊞ *F–G4*

ST PAUL'S BAY

(⊞ *J6*) **Look on the positive side: it's better that the Maltese built their largest resort on a rocky peninsula instead of blighting the few sandy beaches with excessive development. St Paul's Bay (pop. 18,000) is the name of the historic centre which is far smaller than the adjoining resort towns of Qawra (pronounced "Aura") and Bugibba (pronounced "Bu-jiba") which have all merged into one conglomeration.**

Together the resorts offer a total of 10,000 beds and an endless choice of restaurants and pubs. Despite the hotel developments, the promenade, which leads all around the peninsula, is extremely pretty, and the *National Aquarium* is worth a visit. There are plenty of buses available to the beaches and to Valletta.

SIGHTSEEING

MALTA CLASSIC CAR COLLECTION

Over 70 classic cars, most dating from between 1950 and 1972, are on show here, all polished to perfection. *Mon–Fri 9am–6pm, Sat 9am–1.30pm | admission 10 euros | Triq it-Turisti | Qawra | classiccarsmalta.com | ⏱ 30 mins*

NATIONAL AQUARIUM 🐟

In this futuristic building on the waterfront, sharks and rays swim above as visitors pass through a glass tunnel. The aquarium has several tanks, some of which depict ancient and more recent shipwrecks. *Daily 10am–6pm, until 8pm in high season | admission 12.90 euros | Triq It-Trunciera | Qawra | aquarium.com.mt*

EATING & DRINKING

BENJAWAN

Do you fancy a bit of spice? Chef and co-owner Miss Benjawan combines herbs and spices which she has flown in all the way from Thailand to create authentic, tasty dishes. *Evenings only, closed Mon in winter | 148 St Anthony Street | Bugibba | tel. 27 04 06 8 | €€*

HUNGRY COW

This US-style eatery offers an unusually broad selection of burgers, tacos and pizzas, as well as hot dogs and spare ribs. *May–Oct daily 9am–4pm, Nov–April 9am–midnight | Pioneer Road | Bugibba | €*

TARRAGON

A destination for gourmets. Marvin Gauci goes out of his way to tantalise the taste buds. He uses molecular cooking methods and his own smoking oven to prepare dishes such as smoked trout served with a "popsicle surprise" made of white chocolate and strawberry ice cream. The chef coats some of his desserts in frozen fondants that are served at -196°C. *Mon–Sat dinner only, Oct–May also Sun lunch | 21 Church Street | St Paul's Bay | tel. 21 57 37 59 | tarragonmalta.com | €€€*

INSIDER TIP
Ice-cold desserts

BEACHES

GHAJN TUFFIEHA BAY ★ ☀

This bay is unique on these islands: a 200-m / 656-ft stretch of sandy beach that is totally undeveloped and can only be reached on foot or by boat. There are no beach bars, parasols, houses or hotels to spoil the view. It's reached via a long flight of steps from the north or a 15-minute walk along a footpath from the south – time enough to practise your pronunciation of its name: "a-in too-fee-ha". *7km / 4.5 miles from St Paul's Bay | ▢ G7*

GNEJNA BAY

Not a paradise beach but a popular one among locals thanks to its 200m / 656ft of sand. Primitive boat sheds built by fishermen from Mgarr are used by locals as beach huts. Instead of

Undeveloped Ghajn Tuffieha Bay is only accessible on foot or from the sea

The film set from the 1980 movie *Popeye* is a popular family attraction

a trendy beach bar, the bay (pronounced "Gneh-sha") has two basic snack bars. A good watersports centre (gnejnawatersports.com) offers parasols, water-skis, wakeboards, kayaks, canoes and paddle boats for hire. *10km / 6 miles from St Paul's Bay | ⊞ G7*

GOLDEN BAY

The name of the bay was inspired by the colour of its sand. If you are looking for solitude, this is not the place to swim. The watersports station, parasol rental and beach bars do good business here in summer. You can also hire speedboats to race to the neighbouring bays. A relaxing, tranquil stay is only guaranteed in winter, or if you stay directly above the beach in the luxury *Radisson Blu Resort & Spa hotel. 7 km / 4.5 miles from St Paul's Bay | ⊞ G7*

POPEYE VILLAGE

It might seem crazy, but you can hang out at a former film set and still enjoy a day at the beach. The music is loud,

the beach is crowded with sunbeds and the sea view is framed by a colourful pirate village. Older kids love it! Even without children in tow, it's worth stopping to get a free glimpse of the film set before you drive off again. The best place to get a picture of Popeye Village – a must-have from your trip to Malta **INSIDER TIP Photo opportunity** – is from the steep shoreline on the south side of the bay. *July/Aug and Dec daily 9.30am–7pm, Nov, Jan/Feb daily 9.30am–4.30pm | admission depends on the season 10.50–17 euros, children (3–12 years) 8.50–13.50 euros | popeyemalta.com | 4km / 2.5 miles from St Paul's Bay | ⊙ 2 hrs | ⊞ G6*

WELLNESS

MYOKA GOLDEN SANDS

Although it's located in the luxury Radisson Blu hotel, this spa is open to the public. The best thing about it is the beautiful view of the coast and the sea from the indoor pool and relaxation rooms. *Daily 9am–9pm | Golden Bay | tel. 23 56 11 91 | myoka.com/golden-sands*

THE FISH LOUNGE

You may be familiar with the practice of allowing 100 fish to nibble at your hands and feet from fish spas elsewhere in the world. But here you can opt to let 1,200 fish loose on your whole body in a mini-pool. This unusual experience is more fun if you do it as a couple. *Daily 10am–6pm | 9 euros/15-min foot spa, 49 euros/1-hr whole body spa for two | Mellieha | in the Seabank Hotel (on the waterfront) | tel. 21 57 15 65 | thefishlounge.com*

INSIDER TIP
Fish snacks

NIGHTLIFE

At night, British tourists rule the roost in Qawra and Bugibba. Pubs and sports bars dominate the scene, and most Maltese head elsewhere for a night out.

BLACK 'N' WHITE

Teen pop is on the playlist here. The largest disco in the north of the island is open to anyone 17 years old and above. *Daily in the summer, otherwise Fri/Sat 10pm–4am | Bay Square | Bugibba*

CAFE DEL MAR

A touch of Ibiza on Malta? It may not be quite the same, but the trademark compilations of the original are the perfect accompaniment to the sea

and sunset views on Malta. The island's top designer, Mark Pace, was responsible for the striking white interior. It's just a shame that the infinity pool is closed in the evenings. *Daily April–Oct, otherwise Sat/Sun 10am–midnight | Trunciera Street | Qawra | tel. 22 58 81 00*

AROUND ST PAUL'S BAY

2 MGARR

Approx. 15 mins by car, 35 mins by bus from St Paul's Bay

Mgarr consists of one large church surrounded by a small village (pop. 2,800), and that's about it. So why go there? In order to eat at *Restaurant il-Barri (daily | tel. 21 57 32 35 | €)*. There are no tacky folkloric touches here; instead the modern restaurant, which is also the village pub, serves authentic Maltese home cooking in generous portions at affordable prices. Try the rabbit with pork belly, or a hearty vegetable soup. As long as it won't spoil your appetite, descend 12m / 39ft into the village bunker before you place your order; it's only accessible from the restaurant.

INSIDER TIP
Head underground before you eat

During World War II, the village's inhabitants sought shelter from German bombing raids in the 225-m / 738-ft long tunnel. Today, visitors to the bunker are shown a 10-minute video about the suffering of those years. *9*

GOZO

MALTA'S EMERALD ISLE

A 25-minute ferry trip transports you to another world. Gozo epitomises rural tranquillity. Even in the capital, Victoria (Rabat), which lies in the centre of the island, the most interesting corners are kept traffic-free. Soak up the medieval atmosphere of the citadel or the Italian influence in the town's most beautiful square. Most villages on Gozo are situated on low-lying flat hills with far-reaching views. The surrounding land is used for cultivation, to produce a notably strong wine and other delicacies.

Xewkija's Rotunda

It's easy to reach all parts of the island by bike or bus; hiking is possible too in the cooler months. Gozo has only one beach in the strictest sense of the word, but there are several tiny coves to be found between the steep cliffs. Many visitors to Gozo prefer diving anyway. If you're only here on a day trip, you can explore the main sights easily by hire car. And, as the ferries operate around the clock, you'll have time for a Gozitan dinner, ideally in Xlendi directly on the waterfront, before you leave.

GOZO

Iż-Żebbuġ

5 Marsalforr

L-Għasri

2 Ta' Pinu

L-Għarb
San Lawrenz

3 Dwejra Inland Sea ★

Xagħra 6

Cittadella ★

Ggantija ★

8km, 13 mins

1 Victoria (Rabat)
p. 110

Ta' Kerċem

Il-Fontana

7km, 30 mins

Il-Munxar

8 Xewk

4 Xlendi

Ta' Sannat

MARCO POLO HIGHLIGHTS

★ **CITTADELLA**
Victoria's peaceful castle has good
museums and a wonderful view
➤ p. 111

★ **DWEJRA INLAND SEA**
Beautiful coastal formations and an
idyllic lake ➤ p. 113

★ **GGANTIJA**
The most impressive temple site on the
Maltese islands ➤ p. 116

★ **RAMLA BAY**
Gozo's best sandy beach is not built-up
at all ➤ p.120

☀ ☂ **Ramla Bay ★**

MALTA
Gozo

○ In-Nadur

○ Il-Qala

○ Ghajnsielem

6km, 16 mins ○ L-Imgarr

Kemmuna

MEDITERRANEAN

SEA

1

MALTA

▲

1 km
0.62 mi

Almost at the centre of the island, below the medieval castle hill and its recently renovated citadel, lies the island's capital, *Victoria*. (Don't be confused: it's also known as Rabat.) Tourism is concentrated to the south and north of Victoria in the coastal villages of *Marsalforn* and *Xlendi*. Sandy beaches are scarcer on Gozo than they are on Malta, but those who explore the island will find a series of quiet, unspoiled rocky bays and inlets, where they can sunbathe and swim.

Gozo has probably been settled just as long as Malta. The Neolithic temple of *Ggantija* testifies to this. The well-preserved remains of the temple should not be missed, especially because they are nestled in a beautiful natural landscape. Throughout the Middle Ages, Gozo suffered repeatedly from raids and looting by North African pirates and Turkish fleets, so it's no surprise that by the end of the 16th century the island had been all but abandoned. It was resettled by migrants from Malta and Sicily during the 17th century.

In the same century, the Knights of St John built a number of watchtowers on the coast. As the danger of attack declined, so today's capital, Victoria, grew up beneath the citadel. After suffering such hardship during the Middle Ages, Gozo escaped World War II unscathed. Unlike its sister island of Malta, it was never a target for German or Italian bombing raids.

SIGHTSEEING

1 VICTORIA (RABAT)

How many opera houses does a city need? Gozo shows it is not always a question of size. The tiny capital, Victoria, may only have 6,300 inhabitants, but its two opera houses, the ⚑ *Astra* and the *Aurora*, have a

LIVE LIKE A GOZITAN

On Mallorca, Menorca and other Mediterranean islands, country cottages and farms have been converted into luxury holiday homes for the rich and famous. Similar accommodation options, known locally as *razzetts* are available on Gozo – but they're not for VIPs. They are equipped with modern kitchens and bathrooms, air-conditioning and often a little swimming pool. Some are located at the centre of the village; others occupy secluded locations on the edge of a village or among the fields.

The walls are almost always made of un-rendered Maltese stone; the stairs are usually narrow, and the windows are small to keep out the heat of summer. If you stay in one of these houses, you'll be able to buy your vegetables from travelling vendors and the local shop, drink your coffee in the village bar and perhaps get fresh eggs from your neighbour. In this way, you'll make contact with the locals and gain an insight into authentic Gozitan life. For details of agents, see p.140.

With its small squares, narrow streets and numerous churches, Gozo's capital is a homely place

combined capacity of up to 2,800 spectators. The opera houses are owned by two rival *band clubs* and only host a few shows a year. At other times, locals play billiards in the foyers, which are open all day long. Both opera houses are located on long, straight Republic Street, the city's main shopping thoroughfare, which leads up to the former market square, *It-Tokk*.

This square is the starting point for the climb up to the *Cittadella*. More beautiful, however, is the pedestrian-only Pjazza San Gorg, which has all the effortless charm of an Italian piazza. The two squares are just 80m/250ft apart, linked by Triq San Guzepp.

INSIDER TIP
Transported to Italy

A gleaming modern lift transports visitors up to the ★ *Cittadella* and several centuries back in time. First, take in the highly entertaining multimedia exhibition, which is housed in two grand and suitably atmospheric former water tanks built by the British. In little more than 15 minutes, you will learn all the key information about the citadel and its medieval history. Afterwards, continue up two floors to the castle gate.

Steps, guarded by bronze statues of two popes, lead up to the Baroque cathedral of *St Marija (Mon–Sat 11.30am–4pm | admission 4 euros)*, designed by Lorenzo Gafà at the turn of the 17th century. An optical illusion awaits you inside: look up and you'll see what appears to be a

The cliffs around the Dwejra Inland Sea look other-worldly in the evening sun

magnificently painted dome when, in reality, the ceiling of the church is completely flat. This masterful trompe d'oeil is the work of Sicilian artist Antonio Manuele. The illusion only reveals itself when you continue your tour around the outside of the cathedral.

If you carry on a short distance up the hill to left of the cathedral, you will come to the *Gran Castello Historic House (daily 9am–5pm / admission 3 euros, tickets also valid for the prison and the archaeological museum)*. The complex is, in fact, made up of three houses all built around 1500 in a style typical of the time. A series of short films not only gives a glimpse into

everyday life during this period, but also provides information on traditional Gozitan agriculture. Further up the hill, you come to the highest point of the citadel. Enjoy stunning views across the island from the high *city walls* as you make your way back down to the cathedral. Close by on the square is the *old prison* with a reconstructed medieval pillory in front of the entrance – perfect for an unusual selfie. Inside, visitors will discover centuries-old graffiti carved into the walls of the cells by incarcerated prisoners.

If you want to delve deeper into the island's history, visit the well-signposted *Archaeological Museum*. The Arabic gravestone dating from the

there is a striking 19th-century aqueduct. *7km / 4.5 miles from the ferry port | ⊞ D3*

2 TA' PINU

Virtually all observant Catholics will have heard of Lourdes and will know the story of the Virgin Mary appearing in a vision to a local resident there. But few will know that, 120 years ago, the same thing happened on Gozo at Ta' Pinu. Unlike Lourdes, this Gozitan equivalent has not fallen victim to mass commercialisation, even though a grand neo-Romanesque basilica was built on the site where it happened between 1921 and 1932. Inside the church are many votive offerings, but also crutches and prosthetic limbs left behind by those who have been healed by the miraculous powers of the Virgin. Thousands of locals come here on pilgrimages every year, but when it is free of the crowds, this is a gloriously peaceful place – and the surroundings are perfect for a picnic. *Daily | 12km / 7.5 miles / 25–40 mins from the ferry port | ⊙ 30 mins | ⊞ C2*

3 DWEJRA INLAND SEA ★

Even nature does not last forever. In February 2017, Gozo's most famous attraction, the natural rock arch known as the *Azure Window*, collapsed into the sea and disappeared. However, there is still enough to see and do here to make a visit worthwhile. Thousands of fossilised sea creatures can be found on the rocky shore, and children can splash in the rock pools, some of which are deep enough for swimming.

12th century is well worth seeing. Less appealing perhaps is the display on ancient burial methods. These include a complete skeleton dating from the third to the fifth century lying alongside the amphora vessel in which it was originally buried; a set of miniature sarcophagi used to hold the ashes of the dead; and the ashes of a dead Roman from the first or second century contained within a glass urn.

On the way out of Victoria are a couple of sights that are worth taking in as you continue your trip around the island. On the left-hand side of the road towards Xlendi is an 18th-century washhouse located in a cave in the rocks, and on the road towards Dwejra,

The main attraction, however, is the *Dwejra Inland Sea*, a saltwater lake surrounded by steep cliffs which lies on the other side of the car park. Here, children enjoy jumping from the rocks into the water.

On the shore, simple sheds house fishing boats, which can be hired for short excursions out to sea. The boatmen navigate a narrow tunnel that leads through the cliffs from the lake to the open water beyond. If the sea is reasonably calm, they will continue as far as *Fungus Rock*, a limestone islet protruding from the sea just off the coast. At the time of the Knights of St John, a sponge-like plant, known as *Fungus melitensis*, was found to grow on the rock. It was believed to have healing properties and was used to stem the flow of blood from wounds. Overlooking Fungus Rock on the mainland is the *Dwejra Tower*, built in 1651 and later used as a lookout to prevent anyone accessing the rock and stealing the precious medicinal plants. If the tower's flag is flying, then its exhibition on the history and nature of the area is open. *14km (8 miles) / 20–25 mins from ferry port |* ⊘ *30–40 mins |* ▥ *C2*

▣ XLENDI

There are lots of "normal" places to swim around the world ... and then there's Xlendi. Only Norwegians, who are used to a coastline of fjords and inlets, might expect to find a beach resort in such a location. The tiny village lies at the far end of a long, narrow inlet. Its waterfront is a mere 50m / 164ft wide and even at low tide there's only around 2m / 6.6ft of sand. This means that most people either

Chandeliers illuminate the splendour, pomp and piety of Xaghra's basilica

access the water via the ladders that are located on the flat rocks on the western side of the bay, or stretch out on the former saltpans to sunbathe, overlooked by the 1658 *Xlendi watchtower*.

The eastern shore is too steep for sunbathing, but a path takes you up the cliffs from here to a tiny fishing chapel. Directly behind the village, a green valley stretches 2km / 1.2 miles inland to the island's capital. About halfway along, you will pass Gozo's liveliest summer-only nightclub, *La Grotta* (see p. 121), situated well out of town so as not to disturb the residents. Xlendi is also the only place on Gozo where you can board a boat in summer for a tour around the island. *10km (6 miles) / 40–55 mins from ferry port | ⌁ C3*

5 MARSALFORN

If you don't want to miss out on the fun, stay in this resort, the only one on the north coast. It's where most tourists on Gozo spend their holiday, and it's especially popular with divers. But Marsalforn is also a popular destination for locals on warm evenings and at weekends. They like to stroll along the waterfront and eat at one of the many restaurants by the sea. The only sandy beach in Marsalforn is about 15m / 49ft long and is next to the marina and fishing harbour. No one comes here to sunbathe, only to take a quick dip. The

INSIDER TIP
Great shot!

most photogenic sight in Marsalforn is the salt pans 1km / 0.6 miles to the west of the resort. Hundreds of flat rock pools combine to form a stunning

geometric pattern. On the way, you will pass smooth rock formations that resemble crashing waves – it's like Arizona by the sea. *⌁ E2*

6 XAGHRA

In Xaghra you can spend hours in the cafés and restaurants on the spacious village square and watch the locals going about their business. While you're there, take a closer look at the two clocks on the tower of *Marija Bambina* church: one shows the actual time, but the other is merely a painting and shows the time as a quarter to eleven, meaning that it's wrong for 1,438 minutes every day. It is meant to confuse Satan and prevent him from disturbing Mass. Close by are two unusual private houses which were built above caverns complete with stalactites and stalagmites. The owners make the most of their location by offering guided tours of both the houses above ground and the caves underneath: *Ninu's Cave (18 January Street)* and *Xerri's Grotto (31 Xerri Grotto's Street | both open approx. 9am–1pm and 4–6pm | donations requested)*.

On the outskirts of town, on the way to the temple of *Ggantija* (see p. 116), you will pass Gozo's only remaining windmill, *Ta' Kola*. Most visitors fail to notice this really romantic structure. It was erected in 1725 and now houses a *windmill museum (daily 9am–5pm | admission 9 euros incl. Ggantija). 6km (3.5 miles) / 15–25 mins from the ferry dock | ⌁ E2*

INSIDER TIP
Catching the breeze

⑦ GGANTIJA ★

How did people move these giant slabs of stone 5,500 years ago? According to ancient folklore, a giantess built Ggantija's temples in a single night while cradling her child at the same time. Today, these well-preserved structures are a designated UNESCO World Heritage Site.

The two temple façades are orientated towards the open space in front, and once reached a height of 10m / 33ft. They were concave in shape and came together at an oblique angle.

In front of the façades was a stone bench where sacrifices were placed. The entrance to each of the temples was formed by a narrow passage, flanked to left and right by massive upright stones called orthostats. The floor and ceiling were also made from huge stone slabs.

In front of the entrance to the left-hand temple lies a stone slab with a raised edge. Traces of fire damage indicate that it was used for burnt offerings. On the slab itself is a shallow bowl that held liquid offerings. The orthostat at the back has four pairs of holes placed opposite each other, which suggests that the entrance to the temple could be barred with wooden beams.

The temple interior consists of a broad central passageway with five kidney-shaped chambers that were probably only accessible to the priests and priestesses. It is worth taking a look at the wall that surrounds the double temple on three sides. To construct it, the Stone Age builders piled up enormous stones in alternate vertical and horizontal formation. *June–Sept daily 9am–6pm, Oct–May daily 9am–5pm | admission 9 euros incl. Ta'Kola windmill in Xaghra | clearly signposted from the southern end of Xaghra | 6km (3.5 miles) / 15 min from the ferry port | ⏱ 1–1.5 hrs | ⬚ E3*

⑧ XEWKIJA

Whether faith can move mountains remains to be seen, but it certainly seems to have the power to shift massive stone blocks. Proof is provided by the enormous *Rotunda (Mon–Sat 9.30am–noon and 3.30–5.15pm | elevator to the cupola from the church museum | admission 2 euros)*, which was financed and built by the residents of Xewkija themselves and inaugurated in 1978. With a height of

Were Ggantija's huge stone blocks manoeuvred into place by giants?

75m / 246ft, its dome is believed to be the third-highest in Europe; it is certainly the tallest in the state of Malta.

INSIDER TIP

A grand panorama!

A walkway circles the imposing cupola at a height of 50m / 164ft, far removed from the tour groups down below. *4km (2.5 miles) / 10–20 mins from ferry port* | D–E3

EATING & DRINKING

BOAT HOUSE

Whether you prefer meat or fish, you're in luck at this waterfront restaurant. A table next to the boats; a view of the surrounding cliffs; immaculate service – it's likely you won't want to leave. Carnivores should try the 280g / 10oz Gozitan pork chops, which are marinated and then cooked on a wood-fired barbecue. *Daily | Marina Street | Xlendi | tel. 21 56 91 53 | boathousegozo.com | €€–€€€*

JUBILEE

This café on Victoria's main square resembles an upscale British pub on the inside. The menu offers sandwiches, homemade pasta, Gozitan pastries, salads and pizzas, as well as daily specials of all kinds. Don't miss the apple and pecan tart. *Daily 8am–10:30pm | It-Tokk | Victoria | tel. 21 55 89 21 | cafejubilee.com | €€ | E2*

OLEANDER

Oleander was the first restaurant in Xaghra to serve good food directly on the village square. Maltese locals have been coming here for generations, whenever they fancy a meal out with family and friends. With the village church straight in front of you, it is a beautiful setting to enjoy Maltese cuisine, including deboned quail. *Tue–Sun | Victory Square | Xaghra | tel. 21 55 72 30 | € | ⧉ E2*

SAMMY'S IL-KCINA TAL-BARRAKA

A small restaurant with bags of atmosphere, outside seating and a view of the fishing harbour – perfect for an evening meal. The owners, Tony and Sam Grech, take bookings during the day in the Gleneagles Bar on the floor above. *May–Oct Tue–Sun evening only | Manuel de Vilhena Street | Mgarr | tel. 21 55 65 43 | €€ | ⧉ F3*

TA' FRENC ⚑

A restored 14th-century manor house in a green valley outside Marsalforn is the go-to destination for private parties and fine organic dining. The meat, fish and vegetables are almost entirely from Gozo; the excellent olive oil is imported exclusively from Sicily. Reservations recommended. *April–Dec Wed–Mon, Jan–March Fri/Sat and Sun midday | on the road between Victoria and Marsalforn | tel. 21 55 38 88 | tafrencrestaurant.com | €€€ | ⧉ D2*

TA' KAROLINA

The tables and chairs are set right by the harbour in Xlendi. The menu offers something for everyone: a wide selection of fish and seafood, as well as rabbit, vegetarian dishes and pasta. *March–mid-Nov daily | Marina Street | Xlendi | tel. 21 55 96 75 | €€ | ⧉ D2*

TA' RIKARDU

This family-run restaurant serving authentic Gozitan cuisine is hidden away next to the cathedral in Victoria's historic citadel. You can enjoy home-made ravioli and rabbit, accompanied by wines from the restaurant's own winery, either in the vaulted cellar of the medieval house or on its rooftop terrace. *Daily 10am–9pm | Cittadella | Victoria | tel. 21 55 59 53 | € | ⧉ D2*

THE GRAPES

You won't pay a premium to dine in Gozo's most picturesque square. The Mediterranean and Gozitan dishes are reasonably priced. On summer evenings, the Grapes becomes a popular place to chill-out and does not close until sunrise. *| Piazza Sam Georg | Victoria | tel. 79 47 35 36 | thegrapeswinebar.com | € | ⧉ D2*

SHOPPING

AQUILINA

The perfect store for anyone looking for a souvenir for their kitsch-loving, devout grandma. You'll find the Virgin Mary and other saints in every size and price category imaginable, often with Maltese names. *Pjazza San Frangisk | Victoria | ⧉ D3*

ORGANIKA

The first organic and fair-trade shop on the island was opened by a young

Enjoy stunning views from the caves around Ramla Bay

French couple over a decade ago. Locals come here to buy organic food and cosmetics, while tourists come for the Gozitan jams, olive oil, sea salt, arts and crafts plus fair-trade items from developing countries. *St George's Square | Victoria | ⌘ D3*

TA' DBIEGI

An old barracks now houses a variety of workshops where delicate jewellery and lace, plus leather, wool and clay objects, are made and sold, alongside jams, candles and paintings. *San Lawrenz | on the road to the Dwejra Inland Sea | ⏱ 20–30 mins | ⌘ C2*

BEACHES

HONDOQ BAY

This sand and pebble beach is about 15m / 49ft long and has a fine view across to Comino. *2km / 1 mile, below the village of Qala | ⌘ F3*

MGARR IX-XINI

This narrow rocky cove encompasses the beach of the Ta' Cenc luxury hotel and a concrete area for sunbathing. *2.5km / 1.5 miles below the village of Sannat | ⌘ E4*

Make the most of the hot summer nights in the bars of Marsalforn and Xlendi

9 RAMLA BAY ★ 🌴

This bay is full of life in summer. The long and wide stretch of sand makes it the most attractive beach on the island. However, there are no sun loungers to hire. Simply spread out your towel on the golden-red sand. There's a breathtaking view of the bay from Calypso Cave to the west. Learn about the nature of the area at the information centre run by the Gaia Foundation. *4km / 2.5 miles north of Nadur* | 🗺 *E2*

WIED IL-GHASRI

Swim in a narrow inlet towards the sea! There's hardly room for more than 10 sunbathers on the tiny shingle beach at the inner end of the fjord, but from there it is easy to get into the water. *3.5 km / 2 miles west of Marsalforn* | 🗺 *D2*

INSIDER TIP
Mini-fjord, mini-beach

XWEJNI BAY

A little cove with bizarre rock formations eroded by the waves and offshore rocks that are perfect for diving and jumping. *1.5km / 1 mile west of Marsalforn* | 🗺 *D1*

WELLNESS

KEMPINSKI SAN LAWRENZ

Palms and flowers frame the windows of the Kempinski Spa. Inside, you'll feel as though you've entered another world – or perhaps that you've been transported east to the orient or India. At the heart of the spa

INSIDER TIP
Ayurvedic treatments

is one of the largest Ayurvedic centres in Europe. Every specialist member of staff, from the doctor to the chef, is from the Indian subcontinent. There are 34 different treatments on offer. You can book everything from a 30-minute head massage for 30 euros to a two-week spa programme that includes two hours of treatments, yoga and Ayurvedic catering for 147 euros per day. Give it a try! *San Lawrenz | tel. 22 11 00 00 | kempinski-gozo.com*

NIGHTLIFE

IT-TOKK
Lounge, café and bar with roof garden, serving good Maltese specialities. *Daily | It-Tokk | Victoria | ⊞ D3*

JUBILEE
The place to see and be seen on Gozo: a stylish café-bar that would not seem out of place in London's Soho. It serves good snacks and pasta dishes and hosts live music on some evenings. Self-styled VIPs sit inside while the tourists hang around outside. *Daily | It-Tokk | Victoria | ⊞ D3*

KU CLUB/PYRAMID CLUB
Between November and April, Victoria's two opera houses, the Astra and the Aurora, resemble good-old village discos when Gozo's teenagers come to rock the joint. *Fri/Sat 11pm–4am | Republic Street | Victoria | ⊞ D3*

LA GROTTA
At weekends you'll find half of Gozo dancing the night away in the rocky caves of the Xlendi valley. The natural surroundings and romantic lighting create the ultimate Gozo atmosphere, but the guest DJs come from all over the world. *June–Oct Fri/Sat, Nov–May only on special occasions such as Valentine's Day or carnival or for school parties | 1km /0.6 miles from Xlendi on the road to Victoria | lagrottaleisure.com | ⊞ G3*

INSIDER TIP
Cave party

A GOOD NIGHT'S SLEEP

BEACH, BEACH, BEACH
With balconies overlooking the sea, and the beach just a stone's throw away from the hotel's front door, the *San Andrea (28 Zi. | Xlendi | tel. 21 56 55 55 | hotelsanandrea.com | €€ | ⊞ C3)* is as good as it looks. Breakfast is served in the hotel's restaurant on the waterfront.

PEACE AND QUIET
Located off the beaten track, *Ta'Cenc (83 Zi. | tel. 22 19 10 00 | tacenc.com | €€€ | ⊞ D3)* is a spacious bungalow hotel, with an established garden and a small spa for guests. It is a favourite haunt of celebrities because of its secluded location on the outskirts of Sannat. Some of the single-storey bungalows resemble Apulian *trulli*. If you prefer to swim in the sea rather than in the hotel's pools, a shuttle bus can take you to a tiny rocky cove just 2km / 1.2 miles away.

DISCOVERY TOURS

Do you want to get to know the special features of a particular region? Then Marco Polo's discovery tours are just the ticket!

① MALTA AT A GLANCE

> ➤ Opportunities for hiking, walking and swimming
> ➤ Impressive prehistoric sites and imposing churches
> ➤ Sea caves and coastal cliffs as well as a boat trip

📍 Sliema ferry port 🏁 Sliema ferry port

🔄 135km / 84 miles 2 days (5 hrs total driving time)

ℹ️ The route is designed as a figure-of-eight so that you can return to your hotel for the night after the first day's itinerary. Valletta and Mdina/Rabat are best visited individually and can be reached by public bus, so they're not part of this tour.

Old Theatre Street, Valletta

THE HEIGHT OF MEGALITHIC CULTURE

This round trip begins in ❶ Sliema, at the ferry port, *on the coastal road between St Julian's and Valletta,* which is where most of the holiday hotels are located. The road rounds a number of bays, then leaves the coast shortly before Valletta and begins to climb slightly uphill; you will see a park on the left-hand side. The dual carriageway passes under a bridge. Shortly thereafter, *turn left, following the signs to Marsa and Paola.* Drive through Paola and follow the signs to the temple of ❷ Tarxien ➤ p. 65.

FISHING IDYLL

After touring the temple, *return to the main road and head towards Marsaskala* ➤ p. 79. Continue *along the southern coast of Marsaskala Bay to St Thomas Tower and then on to St Thomas Bay,* where the road begins to lead inland. At the Bir ir-Deheb roundabout, *turn towards Birzebbuga and then left just afterwards* to ❸ Marsaxlokk ➤ p. 74, the most photogenic seaside town on the whole island. Stroll through the market and stop for a cup of coffee on the waterfront to watch the colourful Maltese fishing boats, known as *luzzi.*

DAY 1
❶ Sliema ferry port

9km   8 mins
❷ Tarxien

18km   25 mins

❸ Marsaxlokk

123

LIGHT SHOWS AND ANCIENT TEMPLES

Follow the coastal road along Marsaxlokk Bay towards Birzebbuga ➤ p.76, continuing until you come to the entrance to the *container ship port at Kalafrana, where the road turns away from the sea*. The road passes through the Hal Far industrial park en route to Zurrieq and, from there, leads down to ❹ Wied iz-Żurrieq. Try to arrive around 1pm, in time to have lunch at the Step-Inn *(daily | €)* before hopping aboard a boat to sail along the cliffs to the ❺ Blue Grotto ➤ p.79 with its fascinating light effects. Afterwards, *drive up the steep coast and turn left* to get to the impressive temples of ❻ Hagar Qim and Mnajdra ➤ p.76, situated in a beautiful natural setting. After your visit, *continue along the little lane to the Tal Bajjada roundabout and then down to the small bay of* ❼ Ghar Lapsi ➤ p.93. Take a seat on the terrace of the Restaurant Blue Creek *(closed Tue/Thu)* and imagine you're on the foredeck of an ocean liner. Next, drive via Siggiewi back towards urban Malta at Hamrun. You can join the motorway here to reach either the ferry dock in ❽ Sliema or your holiday accommodation.

INTO RURAL MALTA

On the second day, *the route begins again at the Sliema ferry dock. This time, follow the coastal road in the opposite direction around Sliema and Balluta Bay.* Just a few kilometres beyond St Julian's, you will once again find yourself in more rural surroundings. Leave the large tourist centre of Bugibba to your right and *circle around St Paul's Bay* on your way into the little town of ❾ Mellieha ➤ p.100. Park either on the sloping main street or directly in front of the church of St Marija. Once you have visited this pilgrimage site with its miraculous depiction of the Virgin Mary and quaint museum, *drive down* to Mellieha Bay ➤ p.101. At the roundabout, *turn south towards Valletta and then turn right after just 100m / 328ft* to ❿ Popeye Village ➤ p.104. The set, which was used for the *Popeye* film, is perfect for a photo! Afterwards, *return to the main road and follow it until you reach a minor road that branches off to the right,* passing through an utterly

15km 16 mins

❹ **Wied iz-Żurrieq**

1km 7 mins

❺ **Blue Grotto**

2km 12 mins

❻ **Hagar Qim and Mnajdra**

5km 20 mins

❼ **Ghar Lapsi**

16km 20 mins

❽ **Sliema**

DAY 2

20km 20 mins

❾ **Mellieha**

3.5km 6 mins

❿ **Popeye Village**

6.5km 7 mins

rural landscape to *Manikata* and then on to **⑪ Golden Bay ➤ p. 104**. You can finally hit the beach! The fine sand is a perfect for sunbathing, or you can swim in the sea, or just have a drink at the beach café. Alternatively, take an hour-long speedboat trip to some of the neighbouring bays.

STEEP CLIFFS AND CART TRACKS

Then it is time for a country-style lunch on the village square in **⑫ Mgarr ➤ p. 105** at *Restaurant il-Barri*. For a truly Maltese meal, choose the rabbit dish, and don't forget to visit World War II bunker which can be accessed from the restaurant. From Mgarr, drive back to

⑪ Golden Bay

3.5km   5 mins

⑫ Mgarr

7km   9 mins

The Maltese nobility left their mark on the architecture of tranquil Mdina

⑬ Mdina

4.5km   8 mins

⑭ Dingli Cliffs

2km   7 mins

⑮ Clapham Junction

1.5km   5 mins

⑯ Buskett Gardens

7km   9 mins

⑰ Mosta

10km   15 mins

① Sliema

the main road and head towards Mdina/Rabat. Shortly before ⑬ Mdina ➤ p. 84, make a stop to take a photo of the town's impressive fortifications from a distance. There's plenty to see and do in Mdina and Rabat, so rather than rushing, plan to visit another day. The driving route continues through the village of Dingli to the ⑭ Dingli Cliffs ➤ p. 90. After a walk along the steep coastline, treat yourself to some first-class coffee and cake at The Cliffs restaurant. Next on the itinerary are the mysterious Bronze Age cart ruts at ⑮ Clapham Junction ➤ p. 91, followed by a shady woodland walk through the neighbouring ⑯ Buskett Gardens ➤ p. 92.

FINISH WITH A GIANT DOME

Once you leave the gardens, pass through Mdina/Rabat again on your way to ⑰ Mosta ➤ p. 94, with its impressive domed Rotunda. Park at the church, from where it's only a few steps to the unique Maltese Ta' Marija ➤ p. 94, which serves up live guitar music to accompany dinner. Afterwards, drive *through Balzan and Birkirkara* to get back to the *motorway*, which you can follow back to the ① Sliema or to your holiday hotel.

> **INSIDER TIP**
> **Traditional dining**

❷ A LONG WALK AROUND VALLETTA

➤ The city's top sights
➤ Unusual places to relax
➤ Fabulous viewpoints over the Grand Harbour

📍 Valletta Bus Terminal   🏁 Valletta Bus Terminal

↻ 3.5km / 2 miles   🚶 1 day (80 mins total walking time)

ℹ️ In the summer it's best to travel to Valletta by bus because parking is scarce and expensive.

ULTRAMODERN ARCHITECTURE MEETS HISTORY

Buses stream into Valletta from all parts of the island, terminating at the new ❶ Bus Terminal in front of the city wall. Try to arrive as early as possible. From here, head a few steps to the north and then cross the new bridge into the old town centre. Your eyes will immediately be drawn to the ❷ Parliament Building on Freedom Square ➤ p. 45, designed by Italian star-architect Renzo Piano and opened in 2015. His design concept also included the adjacent open-air theatre, ❸ Teatru Rjal. Both buildings stand at the head of ❹ Republic Street ➤ p. 44, a lively pedestrian thoroughfare that is often decked in flags. A few shops, such as the Wembley Store ➤ p. 58, have retained their colourful old wooden façades, but most now have a modern appearance. However, conspicuous advertising is prohibited, in order to preserve the historic character of the city, which means that you won't even notice McDonald's until you're standing right in front of it.

❶ Valletta Bus Terminal

❷ Parliament Building

❸ Teatru Rjal
❹ Republic Street

CLASSICAL SOUNDS AND VALLETTA'S SHOWPIECE CHURCH

Every Maltese village has an orchestra, and Valletta has several. They rehearse in the premises of the national philharmonic society, La Valette *(297 Republic Street)*

An unmistakable relic of British rule on Republic Street

and *The King's Own (275 Republic Street)*. Drink an espresso at the bar, just like a local, and

INSIDER TIP Meet a musician

observe a bit of authentic Maltese daily life. You might even be able to listen to a few music students as they practise. Between these two buildings, you will find the ❺ National Museum of Archaeology ➤ p.45, allow 30 minutes for a visit. Afterwards, *continue along Republic Street for a few steps* to reach the visitors' entrance to Valletta's most imposing church: ❻ St John's Co-Cathedral ➤ p.46. A little further along Republic Street is the open space of Great Siege Square and the impressive columned portico of the ❼ Law Courts.

GREAT SHOPS AND MALTA'S TURBULENT HISTORY

The walk continues to Republic Square with its street cafés. Be sure to glance inside café ❽ Cordina *(daily | €)* to admire its interior. It is also famous for ice cream and sweet treats. Duly refreshed, *head on a few steps to Palace Square*, where fountains entertain passers-by every hour on the hour. Dabble your feet in the water to cool down on hot days. The square is dominated by the ❾ Grand Master's Palace ➤ p.47. Plan to spend at least an hour touring the palace and its armoury. If you continue on Republic Street as far as North Street, you will pass several jewellers, such as the ❿ Silversmith's Shop ➤ p.58, that are recommended for their delicate Maltese silverwork. Republic Street ends in front of historically significant ⓫ Fort St Elmo ➤ p.50. *Take a right here* to reach the entrance to the ⓬ Malta Experience ➤ p.50, where you can learn about the long history of Malta in a brief audiovisual presentation. When the show is over, *follow the waterfront road along the Grand Harbour* as far as the ⓭ Lower Barracca Gardens ➤ p.51. This is a

❽ Cordina

❾ Grand Master's Palace

❿ Silversmith's Shop

⓫ Fort St Elmo
⓬ Malta Experience

⓭ Lower Barracca Gardens

great place to watch the ships sailing into the harbour.
Pass through Victoria Gate to re-enter the walled city.
Climb the steps of St John's Street until you come to
⑭ Merchants Street. *Turn left onto Merchants Street* to
reach the ⑮ Auberge de Castille ➤ p. 53, which is the
official seat of the prime minister. *A short detour from
here* will take you to the ⑯ Upper Barracca Gardens
➤ p. 51 and a splendid view over the Grand Harbour.
Enjoy a simple cup of coffee at the kiosk in the gardens
and then take a look at the former fortress ⑰ St James
Cavalier ➤ p. 53, which has been converted into a cultural centre, before you make your way back to the
nearby ❶ Valletta Bus Terminal.

⑭ Merchants Street

⑮ Auberge de Castille

⑯ Upper Barracca
Gardens

⑰ St James Cavalier

❶ Valletta Bus
Terminal

➤ Experience unspoiled nature in peace
➤ Find a heavenly spot for a picnic
➤ Develop a sense of rural Malta

📍 A village square in Mgarr

🏁 Mosta

→ approx. 16km / 10 miles

🥾 4-6 hrs (4 hrs total walking time)

📶 easy

↗ 240m / 787ft

ℹ There's little shade on this hiking route, so start early in summer!
Bus service from Valletta to Mgarr. Return services from Mosta to Valletta, Sliema and Bugibba/Qawra.

❶ Village square in Mgarr

1km 12 mins

❷ Zamitello Palace

4km 50 mins

❸ Bingemma Fort

1km 12 mins

❹ Nadur Tower

1km 12 mins

FORTIFICATIONS TO HONOUR THE QUEEN

Enjoy a second morning coffee in the ❶ village square in Mgarr ➤ p.105. Then start your walk along the tarmacked road, *past the mighty church, towards Gnejna Bay*. Behind the striking ❷ Zamitello Palace, a romantic building from the 19th-century with battlements and a little tower, turn left on to a narrower tarmacked lane that leads up to the Victoria Lines. This succession of British forts is situated on the edge of the central Maltese plateau, directly above the Great Fault, a geological feature that stretches across the island. The English built the fortifications in the late 19th century to protect central Malta against invasion, naming them in honour of the British queen at the time. By 1907, it was clear that they were obsolete from a military perspective. However, with the exception of Mosta Fort, they all served as flak posts for air defence in World War II. The first of these forts that you will come to is ❸ Bingemma Fort. Its drawbridge and the heraldic symbols above the gate are well preserved. The route continues to ❹ Nadur Tower. Located at a height of 245m / 800ft above sea level, it is the highest building on the island.

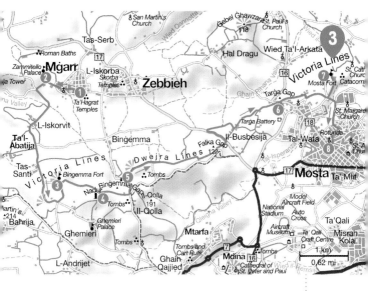

PICNIC SPOT WITH A DIFFERENCE

The next stretch follows an asphalt road to ⑤ Bingemma Gap, one of several passes across the Victoria Lines ridge. Here you will find a small chapel and, below it, several Roman rock graves – it's the ideal spot for a picnic. After two hours' walking, you'll reach the end of the narrow surfaced road along the Victoria Lines and join the wide main road between Mosta and Mgarr, which is on several bus routes. Follow this road *to the left in the direction of Mgarr for about 350m / 0.2 miles and then head off to the right* on a track across the fields. This path leads to ⑥ Targa Gap and the artillery position called Targa Battery. About a kilometre to the north, you will already be able to see ⑦ Mosta Fort. Look for the cave chapel and the former ammunition store in the caves below the fort. From the fort, the final stretch of the walk is via a surfaced road to the town of ⑧ Mosta ➤ p. 94, where you can catch a bus back to Valletta, Sliema or Bugibba/Qawra.

⑤ **Bingemma Gap**

5.5km   70 mins

⑥ **Targa Gap**

2km   25 mins

⑦ **Mosta Fort**

2km   25 mins

⑧ **Mosta**

④ EXPERIENCE ANOTHER WORLD: A DAY ON GOZO

> ➤ Explore steep cliffs and Neolithic temples
> ➤ Discover the beauty of Gozo's capital city
> ➤ Take to the water by kayak or jet ski

📍 Mgarr ferry port on Gozo

🏁 Mgarr ferry port on Gozo

🔄 47 km / 29 miles on Gozo

🚗 1 day (2 hrs total driving time on Gozo)

ℹ️ Avoid the crowds by arriving on Gozo before 9am. Ferries make the crossing from Malta throughout the day and night, and you only pay on the return journey from Gozo. The crossing takes approx. 30 mins.

PANORAMIC VIEWS AND CALYPSO CAVE

① Mgarr ferry harbour

4km   5 mins

The route begins on Gozo at ① **Mgarr ferry harbour**, where all the car ferries from Malta arrive. Take the road from the terminal, then *turn left towards Victoria (Rabat) at the first junction. Follow the main island road through Ghajnsielem and then follow signs to* ② Xewkija ➤ p.116. Park at the Rotunda and climb up to the domed roof to enjoy your first expansive view over this little island. Once you've taken in the panorama, *return to the main road and follow it in the direction of the island's capital.* After a short distance, turn off to the right towards Xaghra. At the lower entrance to the village is the temple site of ③ Ggantija ➤ p.116. Leaving the temple behind, *pass the windmill* on your way to the village square at ④ Xaghra ➤ p.115, where you can take a coffee break in a number of old-style bars. Right next to the village church, *a signpost points the way* to ⑤ Calypso Cave and the best panoramic view over the reddish sands of Ramla Bay ➤ p.120. From here, drive *down to the seaside village of* ⑥ Marsalforn ➤ p.115, and stop for a good lunch around noon at Otters *(St Mary's Street | €€)*, a lounge-restaurant directly on the waterfront.

NSIDER TIP

Climb onto the church roof

TOUR THE ISLAND'S CAPITAL ON FOOT AND THEN HEAD OFF TO THE SOUTH COAST

The next destination on the route is the island's capital, ⑦ Victoria (Rabat) ➤ p.110. Park at the car park next to the bus station, close to the centre of town – to get there from Marsalforn, *cross the broad main road from Victoria and then turn immediately left.* After a thorough exploration of the Cittadella, *drive south to the coast at* ⑧ Xlendi ➤ p.114, where you can go for a swim, hire a motorboat or a jet ski for a thrilling race across the waves or choose a more sedate paddleboat or rowing boat. *The route then continues westwards via Victoria.* It is worth making a short detour to ⑨ Ta' Pinu ➤ p.113, with its lovely and secluded pilgrimage church before you head to the ⑩ Dwejra Inland Sea ➤ p.113; it's separated from the sea by nothing more than a rocky cliff. From there, take the direct route back to Victoria (Rabat) *to eat a delicious dinner at* ⑪ Jubilee ➤ p.117, a café right on the main square, before you make your way to ① Mgarr ferry harbour.

② **Xewkija**

3.5km   10 mins

③ **Ggantija**

1km   2 mins

④ **Xaghra**

2km   3 mins

⑤ **Calypso Cave**

4km   5 mins

⑥ **Marsalforn**

5km   8 mins

⑦ **Victoria (Rabat)**

5km   10 mins

⑧ **Xlendi**

6km   12 mins

⑨ **Ta' Pinu**

4km   8 mins

⑩ **Dwejra Inland Sea**

6km   12 mins

⑪ **Jubilee**

6.5km   12 mins

① **Mgarr ferry harbour**

⑤ GOZO'S BEAUTIFUL COASTLINE: A HIKE FROM MARSALFORN TO GHASRI

➤ Enjoy Gozo's art at your leisure
➤ Swim in a hidden fjord
➤ Take in the fascinating geometry of the saltpans

📍	Marsalforn harbour	🏁	Marsalforn harbour
🔄	7km / 4 miles	🚶	3–4 hrs (2 hrs total walking time)
📶	very easy	↗	230m / 755ft

ℹ There is no shade on this walk, so it's best to set out no later than 8.30am. A day ticket for the buses is 1.50 or 2 euros. Bus timetables are available on *maltabybus.com*.

FAIRYTALE ROCK FORMATIONS

This tour begins at ❶ Marsalforn harbour ➤ p.115. Walk along *the shore road in a westerly direction*. First you will come to Qbajjar Bay, which is still part of Marsalforn, and then ❷ Xwejni Bay ➤ p.120, with its fantastic rock formations. They resemble crashing waves that have been turned to sandstone.

SALTPANS AND A MINI FJORD

This is also the start of the rocky plateau that lines the shore, where locals have been harvesting salt for generations from salt pans cut directly into the rock. Try and balance your way across the narrow ledges between the pools. The geometric shapes created by the salt pans are likely to inspire you to take some abstract photographs. Follow the path inland, away from the sea, and then take the *short footpath that leads down to the right to a beach* no bigger than a room in a house. The beach lies at the head of a 100-m / 328-ft long and very narrow miniature fjord, known as ❸ Wied Il-Ghasri ➤ p.120, that winds its way towards the sea.

---

❶ Marsalforn harbour

2km   25 mins

❷ Xwejni Bay

2km   25 Mins

❸ Wied Il-Ghasri

SNORKELLING OR SUNBATHING?

INSIDER TIP
Alone in the fjord

You can go snorkelling here, or you could swim through the inlet from the beach to the sea and enjoy the peaceful tranquillity. Only very few tourists make their way here as there is no beach bar and no parasol hire. Once you're *back on the main trail, keep right at the next fork* and follow the little piles of stones that mark the boundaries of the fields here. After 30m / 100 ft, *turn left onto a wide path, heading uphill.* To the right, beyond the cacti fields, look out for the lighthouse and the village church in ❹ **Ghasri**, which is the final stop on this walk. The village square also has a little café where you can sit and relax until the bus comes. You will have to *change buses in Victoria (Rabat)* in order to get back to ❶ **Marsalforn harbour**.

❹ **Ghasri**

❶ **Marsalforn harbour**

Locals still gather salt from the Roman saltpans at Xwejni Bay

GOOD TO KNOW

HOLIDAY BASICS

ARRIVAL

GETTING THERE

Flights to Malta from the UK are operated by Air Malta, BMI, Easyjet, Jet2, Ryanair, TUI and Wizz Air from London airports and some regional hubs. There are also flights from many airports on the European continent operated by Air France, Alitalia, Lufthansa and others. Flying time from the UK is just over three hours. All flights arrive at the state-of-the-art *Luqa International Airport*. Bus services X1 to X4, plus 119, 135, 201 and 217 all depart from here to destinations around the island, including the ferry port at Cirkewwa. Tickets can be bought in the terminal or on the bus.

INSIDER TIP
Shuttle Service
A reasonably priced alternative is a transfer by minibus. These can be booked in advance by phone or online, or they can be arranged at the Malta Transfer desk in the baggage reclaim hall (*e.g. to Bugibba approx. 10 euros, to Cirkewwa approx. 12 euros | tel. 79 64 64 81 | maltatransfer.com*).

At the taxi information stand in the arrivals hall, you can book a taxi for a fixed price (*e.g. to Valletta 17 euros, Sliema 20 euros, Bugibba 28 euros and Cirkewwa 35 euros | gettinghere. maltaairport.com*).

If you want to arrive by boat, you can catch a fast catamaran service from Italy. The catamarans transport vehicles up to 2.2m / 7.2ft in height and sail up to 12 times a week in summer and three or four times a week in winter from the Sicilian ports of Pozzallo and Catania. Information is available from *Virtu Ferries (Xatt il-Ghassara tal-Gheneb | Virtu Passenger Terminal | tel. 22 06 90 22 | virtuferries.com*).

Cycling at Xwejni Bay, Gozo

GETTING IN

As the Republic of Malta is a member of the EU, travellers from other EU states need only an ID card or passport, and children below the age of 12 need a children's passport or ID card. Citizens of the UK, Canada and the USA need a valid passport but no visa if they are travelling as tourists for a period of not more than 90 days.

CLIMATE & WHEN TO GO

Thanks to its many historic sights, Malta is not a seasonal travel destination. Hotels, restaurants, language schools and souvenir shops stay open all year round. The countryside is at its most colourful in spring; this is also when the water temperature of the Mediterranean starts to rise above 18°C / 64°F. Holidaymakers become less active in July and August when the thermometer can reach temperatures of 35°C / 95°F and above. It remains

Adapter Type G

240 V alternating current; British-style three-pin plugs. Adapters are widely available for any devices using different plug types.

warm enough to swim in the sea until November. Advent on Malta is a festive time to visit: coloured lights decorate the streets and loudspeakers play Christmas carols.

GETTING AROUND

BUS

The public bus network is excellent on Malta and Gozo. Tickets are extremely cheap; the website *publictransport.com.mt* provides up-to-the-minute information. A single ticket (valid for up to two hours) costs 1.50 euros in winter and 2 euros between mid-June and mid-October. Night service tickets cost 3 euros all year round. A weekly pass for all lines costs 🐷 21 euros (children up to ten years pay 15 euros).

Single tickets can be purchased from the driver. Weekly passes are available from the bus company offices in the airport's arrival lounge as well as at the bus terminals in Valletta, Bugibba, Victoria (Gozo) and Sliema ferry port and in many shops and lottery ticket kiosks. Accurate timetables can be found at all bus stops; display screens and announcements on the bus indicate the next stop as you travel around.

More comfortable, albeit more expensive, are the hop-on, hop-off buses run by *Malta Sightseeing (tel. 21 69 49 67 | maltasightseeing.com)*. The open-top double-decker buses travel on two routes around Malta (northern Malta: blue; southern Malta: red) and one on Gozo (green), and take in many of the most interesting tourist destinations on the islands. On board, information (in 16 languages) is provided via headsets.

A day ticket for each bus route costs 20 euros, including a transfer to and from your hotel to one of the stops. The buses run every 30 minutes on Malta, starting from Sliema ferry port, and every 45 minutes from Victoria on Gozo. During the summer season, an additional "Malta by Night" tour is available.

FERRIES
In summer there are 33 sailings daily between Cirkewwa in northern Malta and Mgarr on Gozo, running around the clock; from November to May this is reduced to approx. 22 sailings between 5.45am and 11.30pm. Crossing time is approx. 30 minutes. You won't be sold a ticket for the crossing from Malta to Gozo; they are only available at the ferry terminal on Gozo and automatically include the two-way trip. A return ticket for one person costs 4.70 euros, or 1.20 euros for children (3–12) and bicycles; a car with driver is charged 16 euros. For further information, contact *Gozo Channel Company (tel. 22 10 90 00 | gozochannel.com)*.

In high season, little boats go to and fro all day between Mgarr, Comino and Cirkewwa. Passenger ferries run between Sliema and Valletta and between Valletta and Vittoriosa/Birgu. Red shuttle minibuses connect the two ferry docks in Valletta with each other (3 euros) and with the city centre (1 euro).

Water taxis travel between the Valletta waterfront, Vittoriosa and Senglea. You can also hire a traditional *dghajsa* for a romantic private harbour tour. For further information contact *tel. 98 12 98 02 | maltesewatertaxis.com*

VEHICLE HIRE
Rental prices are low on Malta thanks to keen competition among the car-hire companies. The minimum age for hiring a car is 25, and it is sufficient to have a national driving licence. A compact car can be hired for around

12 euros per day and 40 euros per week. It's a good idea to take out comprehensive insurance cover. Always notify the police if you're involved in a road-traffic accident.

Traffic drives on the left. Vehicles coming from the right have priority except at roundabouts where the vehicles that are already on the roundabout have right of way (unless otherwise signposted). Speed limits are 50kph / 31mph in built-up areas and 80kph / 50mph on country roads. Most drivers obey the rules of the road, as fines for traffic offences are high, starting at 100 euros. The main roads are in good condition, but side roads are often full of potholes. The maximum permitted blood alcohol limit is 0.5g per litre (or 0.2g per litre for new licence-holders and commercial drivers).

TAXI
Several independent taxi companies operate on Malta. It is unusual to hail a taxi on the street; instead, book your ride in advance or hop in at one of the cab ranks. Prices are comparable to most other European countries.

ORGANISED TOURS
Half-day and full-day coach tours with officially licensed guides are on offer all year round. There are also half-day excursions to Valletta, including the Co-Cathedral, museums and the Malta Experience (approx. 37 euros), or to Mdina, including the Dingli Cliffs and San Anton's Gardens (approx. 27 euros).

Other options include full-day tours to Gozo (from 55 euros) or across the south of the island with stops at the temples of Hagar Qim and Marsaxlokk (approx. 52 euros); evening tours to Mdina, and organised trips to festivals (approx. 18 euros). Prices for full-day tours usually include admission to the sights, lunch and a transfer.

In addition to the coach tours, less environmentally friendly jeep tours are available (from approx. 50 euros for a full day), as well as boat trips to destinations as far away as Sicily. It pays to compare prices as the competition between operators is fierce.

EMERGENCIES

CONSULATES & EMBASSIES
British High Commission
Whitehall Mansions | Ta' Xbiex Seafront | Ta' Xbiex XBX 1026 | tel. 23 23 00 00 | ukinmalta.fco.gov.uk

Consulate of Canada
103 Archbishop Street | Valletta, VLT 09 | tel. 25 52 32 33 | canhcon@demajo.com

Irish Embassy
Whitehall Mansions | Ta' Xbiex Seafront | Ta' Xbiex XBX 1026 | tel. 21 33 47 44 | dfa.ie/irishembassy/malta

US Embassy
Ta' Qali National Park | Attard, ATD 4000 | tel. 25 61 40 00 | mt.usembassy.gov

EMERGENCY SERVICES
Call 112 – for access to police, fire brigade and eand ambulance.

HEALTH

The standard of medical care is generally good on both islands. Although the European Health Insurance Card for EU nationals and Global Health Insurance Card are both accepted, you are strongly advised to take out additional comprehensive travel health insurance. Citizens of Canada and the USA should ensure that they have medical insurance that covers their whole trip to Europe.

Pharmacies are open Mon–Sat 8.30am–1pm and 4pm–7pm. Refer to the newspapers for details of after-hours medical services.

No special health precautions are necessary for Malta beyond protecting yourself from the Mediterranean sun and high temperatures. If you want to swim from the rocky coast, it is advisable to wear bathing shoes to protect your feet against sea urchins. The tap water on Malta is fine for cleaning your teeth but doesn't taste great.

ESSENTIALS

ACCOMMODATION

If you're looking to stay somewhere a little bit different, book a *razzett*, one of the traditional rural holiday houses on Gozo – see p. 110, Live like a Gozitan *(gozovillageholidays.com, gozofarmhouses.com)*. Or rent out an apartment in a historic palazzo in Valletta *(livingvalletta.com, vallettavintage.com)*, or book a room in the only hotel in Mdina located inside the city walls *(xarapalace.com.mt)*. The IYHF youth hostels in Malta are located in Bugibba, Sliema and Gzira and in Ghajnsielem on Gozo. For more information enquire at NSTS *(220 St Paul Street | Valletta | 25 58 80 00 | hihostels.com)*.

BANKS

The euro has been Malta's official currency since 2008. Coins show a Maltese cross and an altar from the prehistoric temple of Mnajdra. ATMs are easy to find in all towns.

CAMPING

There is a campsite on the north coast of Malta: *L'Ahrax tal-Mellieha (Ⅲ H5) (tel. 21 52 11 05 | www.maltacampsite.com | pitches from 15 euros/night, caravan for 4 people from 35 euros/night)*.

CUSTOMS

EU citizens can import and export goods for their own personal use without paying duty. The limits are 800 cigarettes, 400 cigarillos, 200 cigars or 1kg of smoking tobacco; 10 litres of spirits over 22 % vol., 90 litres of wine, 110 litres of beer per adult. Citizens of other countries, e.g. the UK, USA and Canada, can import the following without paying duty: 200 cigarettes, 100 cigarillos, 50 cigars, 250g of tobacco; 1 litre of spirits over 22% vol., 2 litres of liquors or fortified wine, 16 litres of beer; 50g of perfume or 250ml of eau de toilette; and other goods up to a value of 175 euros.

DISCOUNTS

Purchase the ➤ *Malta Discount Card* (20 euros) for good savings at many

FESTIVAL & EVENTS
ALL YEAR ROUND

FEBRUARY/MARCH
Carnival Parades, masquerades and dance competitions take place all over Malta and Gozo; the biggest celebrations are in Valletta (photo).

MARCH/APRIL
Good Friday Large processions are held in 14 villages.
Easter Sunday Magnificent processions take place in Vittoriosa, Senglea and Cospicu.
🏴 **Firework Festival** The display over the Grand Harbour on 29/30 April is best viewed from Barriera Wharf.

MAY
World Music Festival A two-day festival at Fort St Elmo in Valletta.

JUNE
🏴 **Isle of MTV** Europe's biggest free open-air festival sees international pop and rock bands perform on St Publius Square in Floriana.
Mnarja-Fest Music, singing and illuminations in Buskett Gardens on 28 June, then traditional horse races in Rabat the following afternoon.

Victoria International Arts Festival Classical music, tango and jazz on Gozo from mid June to mid July.

JULY
🏴 **Festas** Birkirkara, Fleur de Lys, Hamrun, Luqa, Rabat and Sliema all celebrate with fireworks on the first Sunday of the month.
Malta Jazz Festival Valletta waterfront hosts three days of jazz.

15 AUGUST
Santa-Marija-Feste Celebrations in many villages, including Mgarr, Mosta, Gudja and Qrendi.

SEPTEMBER
Great Siege Regatta Traditional rowing boats take to the waters of the Grand Harbour on 8 September with festivities on shore.
Notte Bianca For one night at the end of the month, the streets, squares, palaces and museums of Valletta host all kinds of live concerts.

OCTOBER/NOVEMBER
Mediterranea Festival Concerts, performances and tours on Gozo.

museums, sights and restaurants (*maltadiscountcard.com*). Even without this card, young people, students and senior citizens over 60 are often entitled to discounted admission to many of the sights. Be sure to carry your personal/student ID with you at all times!

HOW MUCH DOES IT COST?

Espresso	1 euro / £0.85 / $1.16 *for a single espresso in a bar*
Wine	from 10 euros / £8.48 / $11.57 *for a bottle of wine in a restaurant*
Cake	3 euros / £2.54 / $3.47 *for a slice of cake in a café*
Beach	10 euros / £8.48 / $11.57 *for a sunshade and two loungers*
Taxi	1.50 euros / £1.27 / $1.74 *per kilometre*
Fuel	1.30 euros / £1.10 / $1.50 *per litre of unleaded petrol*

Anyone who wants to work their way through the gamut of historical sights and museums should invest in the *Multisite Pass*. It's valid for entry to 27 museums, palaces and archaeological sites on Malta and Gozo for 30 days. It costs 50 euros for adults, 38 euros for students and seniors and 25 euros for children, and can be purchased from *shops.heritagemalta. com*. Holders are entitled to a 10% discount in museum shops too.

INFORMATION
Tourist Information (𝕞 c–d4)
Auberge d'Italie | 28 Melita Street | Valletta | tel. 2 12 20 01 93

Gozo Information Office (𝕞 C4)
17 Independence Square | Victoria | tel. 22 91 54 52

Malta Tourist Authority
In the UK:
Unit C, Park House| 14 Northfields | London SW18 1DD | tel. 020 8877 6991 | visitmalta.com

NATIONAL HOLIDAYS

1 Jan	New Year's Day
10 Feb	Feast of St Paul's shipwreck
19 March	St Joseph's Day
31 March	Freedom Day
March/April	Good Friday; Easter Sunday
1 May	Labour Day
7 June	National holiday
29 June	St Peter and St Paul's Day
15 Aug	Assumption
8 Sept	End of the Great Siege
21 Sept	Independence Day
8 Dec	Immaculate Conception
13 Dec	Republic Day
25 Dec	Christmas Day

OPENING TIMES
Almost all state museums and archeological sites operate standard opening times from 9am to 5pm daily. Find current admission fees and opening times at *heritagemalta.org*.

PHONES & MOBILE PHONE

The country code for Malta and Gozo is 00356. When making a call from Malta, dial 0044 for the UK; 001 for the USA and Canada; 00353 for Ireland; then dial the local code without "0" and then the individual number.

Public phone boxes are becoming increasingly rare on Malta. If you plan to use your mobile a great deal while on Malta, it pays to invest in a Maltese SIM card, available from phone shops such as Vodafone or Go (there are outlets at the airport in the Arrivals hall).

SMOKING

Smoking is strictly forbidden on all Maltese buses, in hospitality venues and in all public institutions. There is an SB smoking terrace at the airport.

TIPPING

In some restaurants service is not included in the bill, in which case you should give the waiter about 10%.

WIFI

Free WiFi hot spots exist in many public spaces around Malta. More and more cafés and bars also offer free Internet access, although hotels may charge for this service.

WEATHER

High season
Low season

	JAN	FEB	MARCH	APRIL	MAY	JUNE	JULY	AUG	SEPT	OCT	NOV	DEC
Daytime temperatures (°C)	15°	15°	17°	19°	23°	28°	30°	31°	28°	24°	20°	17°
Night-time temperatures (°C)	10°	10°	10°	12°	15°	19°	21°	22°	21°	18°	14°	11°
☀ Hours of sunshine per day	6	7	8	9	10	12	12	12	9	7	6	5
🌧 Rainfall days per month	12	7	6	4	2	0	0	1	3	9	10	12
≈ Sea temperature in °C	15°	14°	15°	15°	18°	21°	24°	25°	24°	22°	19°	17°

☀ Hours of sunshine per day   🌧 Rainfall days per month   ≈ Sea temperature in °C

HOLIDAY VIBES

FOR RELAXATION AND CHILLING

FOR BOOKWORMS AND FILM BUFFS

📖 THE KAPPILLAN OF MALTA

Nicholas Monsarrat's book (1977) tells of a humble priest caring for his flock in the catacombs during the bombing raids of World War II, interspersed with older stories of endurance from Maltese history.

📖 THE RELIGION

This best-selling historical novel by Tim Willocks (2006) is a tale of blood and thunder from 16th-century Malta, as the Knights of St John fight desperately to defend the island against the besieging Turkish forces.

🎥 THE COUNT OF MONTE CRISTO

The film adaptation of the adventure classic by Alexandre Dumas was shot on Malta and starred Gérard Depardieu and Ornella Muti (1998).

🎥 MUNICH

Malta played a starring role in Steven Spielberg's 2005 thriller, with small towns transformed into great cities for the big screen: Rabat represented Rome and Athens. The film, starring Daniel Craig, dramatises the Israeli government's retaliation for the attack on its athletes at the 1972 Olympics.

PLAYLIST

0:58

II IRA LOSCO – High
Losco came second in the Eurovision Song Contest 2002 with this song.

▶ MUXU – So Good
The island's best known R'n'B musician comes from Msida.

▶ 215 COLLECTIVE – Feel about it
Rap from Pietá that incorporates elements of international hip-hop.

▶ JOSEPH CALLEJA – Nessun Dorma
The tenor from Attard is Malta's most successful opera singer.

▶ CHIARA – Angel
Achieved second place in the 2005 Eurovision Song Contest.

▶ WEEPING SILENCE – Eyes of the Monolith
This Maltese band performs goth, doom rock and heavy metal.

Your holiday soundtrack can be found on **Spotify** under **MARCO POLO Malta & Gozo**

Or scan this code with the Spotify app

ONLINE

RADIO MALTA
With this app you can tune in live to 35 Maltese radio stations.

TALLINJA
Everything you need to know to navigate the Maltese bus service.

NATURETRUSTMALTA.ORG
The website for environmentalists, conservationists and nature lovers.

ECABS MALTA
Forget Uber, this is the app you'll need to grab a cab on Malta.

LOVINMALTA.COM
An entertaining, high-quality website featuring gossip, lifestyle, food and music.

ALBUMS.VIEWINGMALTA.COM
15,000 photos and over 250 videos on all kinds of themes relating to Malta and Gozo.

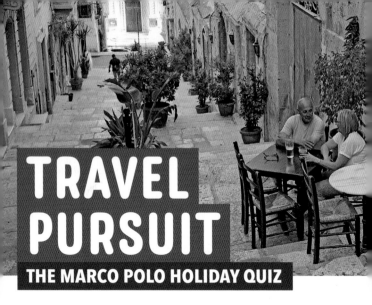

TRAVEL PURSUIT

THE MARCO POLO HOLIDAY QUIZ

Do you know what makes Malta and Gozo tick? Test your knowledge of the idiosyncrasies and eccentricities of the country and its people. You'll find the answers at the foot of the page, with more detailed explanations on pp18–23.

❶ Why do church clocks often show two completely different times?
a) Faulty workings
b) Sloppy workmanship
c) Fear of the devil

❷ Which of these is a booming industry on Malta?
a) Online gambling
b) Excursions by seahorse for singles – but only if they sit side-saddle
c) Temporary nuclear waste storage

❸ What have the Maltese used as the building material for their houses and palaces for the last thousand years?
a) Glass
b) Lego bricks
c) Shell limestone

❹ What is the relevance of *langues* (tongues) on Malta?
a) They're a popular dish, especially when served with red-wine sauce.
b) They were the national groupings of the Order of the Knights of St John.
c) The Maltese like to stick them out, and not just for the doctor.

Answers: 1c, 2a, 3c, 4b, 5c, 6a, 7c, 8a, 9c, 10c

Valletta

❺ Which of these is in short supply on Malta?
a) Beer
b) Wine
c) Drinking water

❻ What is a neolith?
a) A menhir, like the one Obelix always carries around with him in the *Asterix* comics
b) A small car manufactured on Malta
c) A Maltese heavy-metal band

❼ Which Maltese hobby ought to be banned?
a) Stamp collecting
b) Singing
c) Bird-hunting

❽ Which other European country values its EU membership as highly as Malta?
a) Lithuania
b) Poland
c) Hungary

❾ Where does Malta dump all its rubble?
a) In the sea
b) In Tunisia
c) In abandoned quarries

❿ How many students sign up for a place at one of Malta's English-language schools each year?
a) 800
b) 8,000
c) 80,000

DOS & DON'TS!

HOW TO AVOID SLIP-UPS AND BLUNDERS

BE AWARE OF PARKING RULES

On Malta and Gozo, no parking and no stopping zones are often distinguished only by coloured lines on the roadside. White lines mean parking is allowed, whereas yellow lines mean that parking and even stopping are strictly prohibited. Green lines indicate designated parking spaces for local residents; blue lines also indicate parking for residents but only between 9pm and 7am.

DON'T BUY EXOTIC SOUVENIRS

Maltese fishermen don't seem to be bothered when endangered sea turtles get caught in their nets. In fact, in some cases, they sell the shells on the black market. The import of turtle shells to the UK, EU, the USA and Canada is forbidden, as is the import of other animals and animal products protected under the Washington Convention on endangered species (CITES). Steer clear of stuffed fish and birds, and anything made from ivory.

DON'T SUNBATHE TOPLESS

In less strictly Catholic countries the numerous rocky headlands and little coves that are found on Malta would be great places for skinny dipping, but on this island it's best to bathe as if the Pope were watching and keep your costume on.

DON'T GO TO THE ATM TOO OFTEN
It's better to withdraw your holiday money in one go, rather than repeatedly withdrawing small amounts. This is because your bank will charge you for each individual transaction, regardless of the amount.

DON'T BUY OR USE ILLEGAL DRUGS
The sale and possession of hashish and other drugs is illegal and subject to severe penalties. Faced with the fact that Malta is one of the main transit countries for drugs from North Africa to Europe, the Maltese government has responded with draconian measures. Three grammes of cannabis is quite enough to put the user behind bars for six months; expect no mercy from Maltese judges in this matter.

INDEX

WE WANT TO HEAR FROM YOU!

Did you have a great holiday? Is there something on your mind? Whatever it is, let us know! Whether you want to praise the guide, alert us to errors or give us a personal tip – MARCO POLO would be pleased to hear from you.

We do everything we can to provide the very latest information for your trip. Nevertheless, despite all of our authors' thorough research, errors can creep in. MARCO POLO does not accept any liability for this. Please contact us by e-mail.

e-mail: sales@heartwoodpublishing.co.uk

CREDITS

Picture credits
Front cover: View of Upper Barrakka gardens, Valletta (istock/trabantos)
Photographs: AWLimages/John Warburton-Lee: D. Cahir (112/113); K. Bötig (151); DUMONT Bildarchiv: T. Schulze (28); J. Holz (47); huber-images: M. Bortoli (119), G. Cozzi (106/107), R. Schmid (6/7, 54/55, 74, 84, 114, 146/147); M. Kirchgessner (18/19, 64, 120); Laif: G. Hänel (51), A. Hub (136/137); Laif/CAMERA PRESS: C. Molden (10); Laif/Challenges-REA: H. Bigo (61); Laif/Redux: A. Mamo (23); mauritius images: R. Elsen (80/81); mauritius images/age fotostock: C. Goupi (148/149), J. C. Muñoz (66/67); mauritius images/Alamy (26/27, 27, 32/33, 56, 62, 70/71, 103, 111, 126), G. Balfour Evans (77, 105), E. Blanco (12/13), V. P. Borg (89), Ivoha (116/117), J. Kruse (96/97), E. Linssen (11, 24/25), V. Onyshchenko (78), P. Scholey (58/59), R. Scott-Alexander (9), N. Setchfield (30/31), A. Souter (90), K. Sriskandan (31), S. Staszczuk (100), Yegorovnick (front flap outside, front flap inside, 1); mauritius images/Alamy/eFesenko (back flap, 2/3, 94/95, 122/123); mauritius images/Alamy/Live News: A. Adams (128); mauritius images/Alamy/Photononstop: T. Bognar (87); mauritius images/blickwinkel: O. Protze (52/53); mauritius images/CuboImages (92); mauritius images/Imagebroker: Kohls (38/39); mauritius images/imageBROKER: K. F. Schöfmann (20); mauritius images/imagebroker: E. Strigl (135); mauritius images/NPL-Wild Wonders of Europe (35); mauritius images/Prisma/VC-DLH (139); H. Mielke (14/15); Schapowalow: R. Schmid (8, 48); Schapowalow/4Corners: R. Taylor (44). Shutterstock.com: Nowaczyk (148/149)

4th Edition – fully revised and updated 2022
Worldwide Distribution: Heartwood Publishing Ltd, Bath, United Kingdom
www.heartwoodpublishing.co.uk

© MAIRDUMONT GmbH & Co. KG, Ostfildern
Author: Klaus Bötig; **editor**: Marlis von Hessert-Fraatz
Picture editor: Gabriele Forst
Cartography: © MAIRDUMONT, Ostfildern (pp. 36-37, 125, 129, 131, 132, 135, back cover, pull-out map);
© MAIRDUMONT, Ostfildern, using map data from OpenStreetMap, Lizenz CC-BY-SA 2.0 (pp. 40-41, 42-43, 65, 68, 72-73, 82-83, 86, 98-99, 108-109)
Cover design and pull-out map cover design: bilekjaeger_Kreativagentur mit Zukunftswerkstatt, Stuttgart; **page designs**: Langenstein Communication GmbH, Ludwigsburg
Text on the back flap: Lucia Rojas

Heartwood Publishing credits:
Translated from the German by Sophie Blacksell Jones, Susan Jones and Jennifer Walcoff Neuheiser
Editor: Kate Michell
Prepress: Summerlane Books, Bath
Printed in India

MARCO POLO AUTHOR
KLAUS BÖTIG

This travel journalist likes to be on the move, so he appreciates the short distances on Malta and Gozo. And he loves the fact that you can take a culinary world tour in the space of a few kilometres. There's no sleeping on the job because there's always something new to discover around the next corner. Even time travel isn't too demanding here: step back into prehistory by visiting one of Malta's 5,000-year-old temples.